CAMPAIGN • 219

DUNKIRK 1940

Operation *Dynamo*

DOUGLAS C DILDY   ILLUSTRATED BY HOWARD GERRARD

Series editor Marcus Cowper

First published in Great Britain in 2010 by Osprey Publishing,
Midland House, West Way, Botley, Oxford OX2 0PH, UK
44-02 23rd St, Suite 219, Long Island City, NY 11101, USA

E-mail: info@ospreypublishing.com

A CIP catalogue record for this book is available from the British Library.

ISBN: 978 1 84603 457 2

E-book ISBN: 978 1 84908 264 8

Editorial by Ilios Publishing Ltd, Oxford, UK (www.iliospublishing.com)
Page layout by: The Black Spot
Index by Fineline Editorial Services
Typeset in Myriad Pro and Sabon
Maps by Bounford.com
3D bird's-eye views by The Black Spot
Battlescene illustrations by Howard Gerrard
Originated by PPS Grasmere Ltd
Printed in China through Worldprint Ltd.

10 11 12 13 14   10 9 8 7 6 5 4 3 2 1

FOR A CATALOGUE OF ALL BOOKS PUBLISHED BY OSPREY MILITARY
AND AVIATION PLEASE CONTACT:

NORTH AMERICA
Osprey Direct, c/o Random House Distribution Center, 400 Hahn
Road, Westminster, MD 21157
E-mail: uscustomerservice@ospreypublishing.com

ALL OTHER REGIONS
Osprey Direct, The Book Service Ltd, Distribution Centre, Colchester
Road, Frating Green, Colchester, Essex, CO7 7DW
E-mail: customerservice@ospreypublishing.com

www.ospreypublishing.com

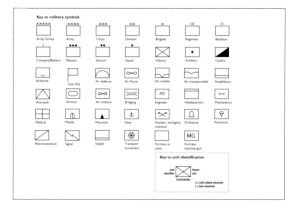

AUTHOR'S NOTE

The author would like to acknowledge his gratitude for the generous
support and assistance of several key individuals. First and foremost I owe
a deep debt of thanks to my wife, Ann, whose constant encouragement
and selfless support throughout the process of writing this complex history
have been indispensable in helping me see it to fruition. Additionally
I thank Mr Peter D. Cornwell not only for his support of this project but
for the products of his lifelong quest to determine what really happened
in the skies of Western Europe in 1940. Peter's exhaustive research and
thorough analysis have finally swept aside the veil of myth, propaganda
and misinformation regarding air combat over France and Britain in that
pivotal year, and I thank him for allowing me to use his comprehensive
data to portray accurately the air battles above Dunkirk. Similarly Mr Don
Kindell is to be thanked for the generous use of his meticulously compiled
and exceptionally detailed database *British and Other Navies in World War 2
Day by Day* (see at www.naval-history.net/xDKWW2-3900Intro.htm).
My thanks, too, to noted historian Dr Don Alberts for his critical review,
corrections and suggestions.

Finally, I am also indebted to a number of experts who assisted in locating
photos necessary to illustrate this book properly. First, to Ian Boyle for
his provision of postcards showing the cross-Channel steamers which
proved so crucial to *Dynamo*'s success (see the Ian Boyle Collection at
www.simplonpc.co.uk) and to Tom Laemlein for his information and
images of the PzKpfw 35(t) in action at Cassel (see Tom's work at
www.armorplatepress.com). As always the Imperial War Museum's (IWM)
photographic archive staff have proven exceptionally helpful in locating
many specific images relating to *Dynamo*. Chief among these are Laura
Clouting, Rosanna Wilkinson and Ian Proctor. At the National Portrait
Gallery, I thank Mr Matthew Bailey for providing images not available from
IWM. Finally, to provide important illustrations of French personalities,
I thank Mme Sophie Massis for her translation assistance and Joan
Boulangé at the Etablissement de Communication et de Production
Audiovisuelle de la Défense. As with Operation *Dynamo* itself, this project
could not have been completed without the combined efforts of many
people and to each of them I give my thanks.

ARTIST'S NOTE

Readers may care to note that the original paintings from which the
colour plates in this book were prepared are available for private sale.
The Publishers retain all reproduction copyright whatsoever.
All enquiries should be addressed to:

Howard Gerrard, 11 Oaks Road, Tenterden, Kent, TN30 6RD, UK

The Publishers regret that they can enter into no correspondence upon
this matter.

THE WOODLAND TRUST

Osprey Publishing are supporting the Woodland Trust, the UK's leading
woodland conservation charity, by funding the dedication of trees.

IMPERIAL WAR MUSEUM COLLECTIONS

Many of the photos in this book come from the Imperial War Museum's
huge collections which cover all aspects of conflict involving Britain
and the Commonwealth since the start of the twentieth century.
These rich resources are available online to search, browse and buy
at www.iwmcollections.org.uk. In addition to Collections Online,
you can visit the Visitor Rooms where you can explore over 8 million
photographs, thousands of hours of moving images, the largest sound
archive of its kind in the world, thousands of diaries and letters written by
people in wartime, and a huge reference library. To make an appointment,
call (020) 7416 5320, or e-mail mail@iwm.org.uk.

Imperial War Museum www.iwm.org.uk

CONTENTS

ORIGINS OF THE CAMPAIGN   5

CHRONOLOGY   8

OPPOSING COMMANDERS   11
Allied commanders . German commanders

OPPOSING FORCES   15
Allied forces . German forces . Orders of battle

OPPOSING PLANS   27
Operation *Dynamo* . The German plan to deal with the Dunkirk pocket

THE CAMPAIGN   32
The race is on, Sunday 26 May . The Panzers roll, Monday 27 May
The Belgians surrender, Tuesday 28 May . The Luftwaffe strikes, Wednesday 29 May
The Panzers turn away, Thursday 30 May . The biggest day, Friday 31 May
The Luftwaffe's last chance, Saturday 1 June . The French fight on, Sunday 2 June
The British are gone, 3 and 4 June

AFTERMATH   86

THE BATTLEFIELD TODAY   90

FURTHER READING   92

INDEX   95

ORIGINS OF THE CAMPAIGN

We have been defeated... We are beaten; we have lost the battle.
French Premier Paul Reynaud to Prime Minister Winston Churchill, 0730hrs, 15 May 1940

Only four days after Heinz Guderian's Panzers crossed the German frontier and descended into the dark forests of the Ardennes they emerged at Sedan, broke through French defences, and – surprisingly – turned towards the Channel coast. Never in the history of warfare had a campaign between such great and apparently equal forces been decided so swiftly and conclusively as the German conquest of France and the Low Countries in May and June of 1940.

In the Netherlands General der Artillerie Georg von Küchler's Armeeoberkommando (AOK) 18 subdued the Dutch Army and occupied 'Fortress Holland' in five days of hard fighting. Against Belgium and the cream of the Allies' mobile armies – the British Expeditionary Force (BEF) and the French 1ère and 7e Armées – the two Panzer, one motorized and 16 infantry divisions of Generaloberst Walter von Reichenau's AOK 6 crossed the Maas and clashed with French light mechanized divisions in the Gembloux Gap.

Meanwhile, moving stealthily through the dark hills of the Ardennes in southern Belgium were three Panzer corps spearheaded by General der Panzertruppen Heinz W. Guderian's XIX Armeekorps (motorisiert) (AK (mot.)). Practically undetected these appeared on the banks of the Meuse River at Sedan,

RIGHT
A 4-ton lightly armoured British Universal Carrier, towing an Ordnance QF 2-pdr Mk IX anti-tank gun, being welcomed by Belgian civilians as they drive through Herseaux on their way to positions on the Dyle Line. (IWM F4345)

LEFT
Meanwhile, through the Ardennes Forest seven German armoured divisions moved steadily and stealthily towards the Meuse River. Two of these were equipped with confiscated Czech-built Skoda tanks, such as the PzKpfw 35(t) light tank, seen here waiting in a wood near Mayen before the opening of the offensive. (Courtesy of the Tom Laemlein Collection)

Monthermé and Dinant. After the Panzers blasted an 80km-wide (50-mile) breach in the French line, Guderian wheeled to the west while the French 2e Armée recoiled to the south. Consequently, the way was opened for Guderian's XIX, Reinhardt's XLI and Hoth's XV AK (mot.) to charge headlong across Picardy, brushing aside the Allies' scattered and weak rear-area units in their pell-mell dash to the English Channel.

The French shared very few details of this unfolding disaster at the time. But in response Général d'armée Gaston H. G. Billotte, commanding the Allies' Groupe d'armées 1, ordered the three Allied armies in Belgium to withdraw from the Dyle to the Senne, to the Dendre and then to the Escaut in an effort to keep the Panzers from curving in behind their now-open right flank and exposed rear areas. Around midnight on 18/19 May, Gén. Billotte visited the BEF's commander, General Lord Gort, and finally informed him in some detail of the Panzer breakthrough and the fact that 'nine, or probably ten, German armoured divisions' were plunging into the rear areas, apparently headed for the Somme Estuary.

Realizing that he would soon be boxed in on both sides with his back to the sea, the veteran warhorse read the situation accurately and informed the War Cabinet via dispatch that he had three possible options: 1) continue to hold the Escaut Line and await re-establishment of his lines of communication through anticipated Allied counterattacks, 2) withdraw to the Somme to join the new French armies forming there, or 3) withdraw towards the Channel ports upon which his new lifeline depended.

To explore the third contingency, at 0600hrs that Sunday morning, six of Gort's senior staff officers met to begin discussing the feasibility of a retreat to the coast. The duty of developing the concept of operations fell to acting operations officer Lieutenant-Colonel Lord Bridgeman who immediately went to work on it. Working all night and subsisting on chocolate and whiskey, Bridgeman devised a sensible, straightforward and relatively simple plan to fall back to the coast and evacuate from the ports between Boulogne and Zeebrugge.

While the War Cabinet still insisted that Gort 'move southwards upon Amiens… and take station on the left of the French Army' they allowed that even if the ordered movement southwards was successful, there would still be units needing evacuation from the Channel ports. As a precautionary measure, therefore, Vice Admiral Bertram H. Ramsay, Flag Officer Commanding Dover, was instructed to assemble the shipping required and begin the planning for evacuating large numbers of British troops. On 21 May the new *commandant suprême des armées alliées* (Supreme Allied Commander), 73-year-old Général d'armée Maxime Weygand, flew from Paris to visit the commanders of the armies trapped in the 'northern pocket' at Ypres and present his 'plan' for pinching off the German armoured spearhead through simultaneous attacks from the south and the north, thus reuniting the Allied armies. To lead the attack, the BEF was required to pull three divisions out of the line and position them for the advance to the south.

In the meantime, the situation on the western side of the pocket was becoming grave. Within the next 36 hours the 2. Panzer-Division invested Boulogne, the 10. Panzer-Division appeared before Calais and the 1. Panzer-Division had driven across the Aa Canal facing Bourbourg, only 16km (10 miles) from Dunkirk. Also on the Aa Canal the 6. Panzer-Division arrived at Saint-Omer and forced a crossing there and the 8. Panzer-Division was advancing on Aire. At the south end of the line Arras was now invested on three sides and west of the city Rommel's 7. Panzer-Division had crossed the Scarpe, pushing the 3e Division légère mécanique off the heights behind it.

On the eastern side ten infantry divisions of Generaloberst Fedor von Bock's Heeresgruppe B assaulted the Belgians and pushed them back all along the 21km (13-mile) line between Menin and Desselghem, threatening to open a gap on the BEF's left flank near Courtrai. Lieutenant-General Alan F. Brooke, commanding II Corps, was alarmed and demanded reinforcements. As an extra precaution Lt. Col. Bridgeman was ordered to revise the draft evacuation plan, especially now that Boulogne and Calais were unavailable for embarkation. Bridgeman's 'second edition' foresaw the BEF retreating along three parallel routes to the coast and being lifted from the 43km (27 miles) of beaches between Dunkirk and Ostend.

On 25 May the strategic situation for the BEF went from grave to desperate. This was occasioned first by the news that at least two divisions would be needed to plug the 13km-wide (8-mile) hole currently being blasted in the end of the Belgian line. Later Gort learned that the planned attacks from the south had been cancelled and the French were instead establishing a linear defence along the Somme, abandoning the prospect of re-linking the two halves of the Allied armies. At 1730hrs he was informed that the French commitment to the northern forces' southwards attack was reduced to merely one division, dooming it to failure.

Confronted by all these factors, Lord Gort made the most momentous decision of his long and illustrious military career, and one – flying in the face of guidance from his civilian masters and military superiors – that was most fateful for the future of the British Army and his nation. After an hour of personal deliberations, he ordered the next day's attack to the south cancelled and the 5th and 50th Divisions moved north to close the breach on the north end of his eastern front, thus denying the Germans an unchallenged advance to Dunkirk and thereby protecting the BEF's avenue of retreat.

CHRONOLOGY

1939

1 September   Germany invades Poland, beginning World War II.

3 September   Britain and France declare war on Germany.

10 September   British Expeditionary Force (BEF) begins arriving in France.

17 September   The Soviet Union invades Poland from the east.

27 September   Warsaw surrenders.

9 October   Hitler's War Directive No. 6 orders the OKH to begin planning for the invasion of France and the Low Countries.

19 October   The OKH produces Aufmarschanweisung *Fall Gelb* (Deployment Directive *Case Yellow*) for the Western offensive. Revised version produced ten days later.

30 November   The Soviet Union attacks Finland. The Allies begin planning to aid Finland, through Norway and Sweden if necessary.

1940

18 February   Generalmajor Franz Halder delivers to Hitler a completely rewritten draft OKH plan placing the *Schwerpunkt* (main weight) of the attack through the Ardennes.

12 March   Finland accepts Soviet terms, ending the Winter War.

20 March   Général d'armée Gamelin, Supreme Allied Commander, adopts 'Breda Variant' of the Dyle Plan designed to meet the German invasion in Belgium while the Maginot Line holds the French frontier.

21 March   Paul Reynaud replaces Daladier as French premier following the failed Allied efforts to aid Finland.

9 April   Germany invades Denmark and Norway. Denmark capitulates that morning. Norwegian capital Oslo and five major ports are occupied.

2/3 May   British forces sent to defend Norway are defeated in detail and evacuated from Åndalsnes and Namsos.

9 May   Chamberlain resigns following the failure of British intervention in Norway. Winston Churchill named Prime Minister of Britain the next day.

10 May   *Fall Gelb* – German invasion of the West – begins.

11 May   BEF and French 1ère Armée arrive at their positions along the Dyle Line.

12 May   Battle of Gembloux – German Panzers clash with French armoured cavalry in central Belgium.

13/14 May	Battle of Sedan – Guderian breaks through French defences. French forces withdraw precipitously, and three Panzer corps head for the coast.	**23 May**	Rear GHQ is evacuated through Boulogne. BEF placed on half rations.
14 May	The Netherlands capitulates.	**23–26 May**	The 10. Panzer-Division invests Calais: the 30th Brigade is ordered to hold to the last. The garrison (3,500 British and 16,500 French troops) surrenders on the 26th.
17–19 May	Général de brigade de Gaulle's feeble armoured counterattacks have no effect on the German 'drive to the sea'.	**24 May**	The OKH orders Heeresgruppe A to halt along the Canal Line.
18 May	BEF GHQ orders non-essential personnel evacuated.	**25 May**	Belgian line is pierced near Courtrai, threatening BEF left flank, and Gort orders two divisions to plug the gap. French Général d'armée Antoine Besson (Groupe d'armées 3) cancels counterattack from the south. Dunkirk is devastated by heavy Luftwaffe attacks.
19 May	BEF, French 1ère Armée and Belgians establish a new defensive line on the Scheldt/Escaut River. Reynaud dismisses Gamelin, appoints Gén. Weygand as the Supreme Commander of Allied Forces. First discussion between BEF GHQ and War Office regarding possibility of retreat to Dunkirk.		
20 May	Guderian destroys most of British 12th and 23rd Divisions (ill-equipped LOC troops) at Albert, Amiens and Abbeville. Reaching English Channel at Noyelles, Panzers cut off all Allied forces in the north. Dover Command planning for evacuation of British forces from Channel ports begins.	**26 May**	Général d'armée Blanchard orders retirement to a large perimeter around Dunkirk. At 1857hrs Operation *Dynamo* ordered to commence. The Oberkommando des Heeres (OKH) orders Heeresgruppe A to resume the offensive
21 May	BEF armoured spoiling attack at Arras. BEF air component evacuates to England.	**27 May**	Operation *Dynamo* begins; 7,669 troops saved. Luftwaffe completely destroys Dunkirk harbour.
22 May	Churchill meets with Reynaud and endorses Weygand Plan for closing breach between Arras and Péronne. Panzergruppe Kleist is transferred to Kluge's AOK 4; Guderian's Panzers advance on Boulogne and Calais.	**28 May**	Belgian Army surrenders. At Dunkirk 17,804 troops rescued. Hitler signs deployment directive for *Fall Rot*. In Norway, Allied forces retake Narvik.
22–25 May	The 2. Panzer-Division invests Boulogne; the 20th Guards Brigade is evacuated by sea on the 23/24th; 4,368 men saved. The remnant of French 21e Division d'infanterie holds out until the 25th.	**29 May**	Luftwaffe launches 'maximum effort' sinks 25 vessels. Kriegsmarine sinks two RN destroyers. French Army joins in the evacuation: 47,310 troops saved. Deployment directive *Fall Rot* is distributed, realignment of Wehrmacht commands begins and Panzers are withdrawn from operations against Dunkirk.
		30 May	Bad weather prevents Luftwaffe interference; 53,823 troops evacuated. Kriegsmarine sinks one French destroyer and severely damages a second.

31 May   French 1ère Armée surrenders at Lille, 35,000 troops captured. Biggest day for *Dynamo*; 68,014 troops rescued.

1 June   Weather clear; Luftwaffe's biggest day; one French and three RN destroyers and 27 other vessels sunk. 64,429 troops evacuated.

2 June   26,256 troops saved. Evacuation of BEF complete.

3 June   26,746 French troops evacuated. Luftwaffe launches Operation *Paula*, a maximum offensive against French air forces around Paris.

4 June   Last night of *Dynamo*; 26,175 French troops saved; later that day 40,000 French troops surrender.

4–7 June   Evacuation of Allied forces from Narvik.

5 June   *Fall Rot* – final conquest of France – begins.

22 June   France signs Armistice with Germany, the battle of France is over, the Battle of Britain is about to begin.

OPPOSING COMMANDERS

I have no confidence in his leadership. When it came to handling a large force, he seemed incapable of seeing the wood for the trees.
Lieutenant-General Alan F. Brooke commenting on his commander,
General Lord Gort, BEF Commander-in-Chief

ALLIED COMMANDERS

Born John Standish Surtees Prendergast Vereker in Ireland in 1886, the leader of the British forces in France succeeded his father to peerage as the 6th Viscount Gort of Limerick in 1902 and entered the British army as **Lord Gort**. Three years later, after completing his education at Harrow, he was commissioned in the Grenadier Guards. During World War I he served as an operations officer on the GHQ staff before returning to the front lines where he commanded the 4th, then the 1st Battalions of the Grenadier Guards. Wounded four times he was awarded the Victoria Cross and two Distinguished Service Orders.

General Lord Gort, on the occasion of being awarded the French grand croix de la Légion d'honneur by Général d'armée Alphonse-Joseph Georges, Commander of Allied Forces North-western France, on 8 January 1940. (IWM F2088)

A large burly man, Lord Gort had the well-earned reputation of being indestructible and had the inspiring visage of a born fighter. For these reasons, in 1937 when theatrical Secretary of State for War Isaac Leslie Hore-Belisha – the 'new broom in the War Office' – wanted renewed interest in the British military, Gort was selected ahead of more senior officers to become the new Chief of the Imperial General Staff (CIGS). The position came with a promotion to full general and since Gort had been a lieutenant-general for only two months, the more senior men he was 'jumped' over were quite naturally piqued. These included General Sir William Edmund Ironside, Lieutenant-General Alan Brooke and Lieutenant-General John G. Dill. Adding insult to injury, Ironside was originally slated to command the BEF, but at the last minute Hore-Belisha appointed Gort instead, and the Viscount's two subordinate corps commanders were Brooke and Dill! Consequently Lord Gort's image suffered grievously from these disaffected officers (even though Ironside and Dill were soon properly placed as CIGS and Vice-CIGS), particularly through the disingenuous characterizations by the ambitious, arrogant and contemptuous Lt. Gen. Brooke, who was joined by others once things began going bad for the BEF.

Subsequently, in large part owing to the disparaging references by these officers, Lord Gort is described by many historians as unimaginative, preoccupied with minutiae and not particularly inspiring. Nevertheless, Gort proved to be a decisive leader with a keen eye for discerning – amidst the chaos and confusion of combat – the critical element and ultimate aim, and had the tireless determination needed to see things through, even if his methods were entirely conventional.

While it was Lord Gort's forthright decision and dogged determination that saved the BEF from destruction, its actual deliverance came through the masterful organizational skills and exemplary leadership of Flag Officer Dover: **Vice Admiral Bertram Home Ramsay**. Son of a Hussars officer, Ramsay joined the Royal Navy in 1898, becoming a midshipman aboard HMS *Cresent* on the North American and West Indies Station. Vigorous, athletic and an ardent sportsman, Ramsay easily overcame his rather slight build with energy, intelligence and self-confidence. During World War I he held successful commands of the monitor *M-25* and destroyer HMS *Broke* in the crack Dover Patrol and participated in the Second Ostend Raid, being mentioned in dispatches. After the war he was promoted rapidly, becoming King George V's naval aide de camp (ADC) and finally the Home Fleet Chief of Staff.

Retiring as a rear admiral in December 1938 over a dispute with his boss, Home Fleet Commander Admiral Sir Roger Backhouse, nine months later Ramsay was recalled as 'Flag Officer in Charge, Dover' because of his extensive knowledge of Channel operations. When that subordinate echelon of the Nore Command was elevated to coequal status, Ramsay was promoted to vice admiral, reporting directly to the Board of Admiralty. At the age of 57, Ramsay still possessed boundless energy, was a cool, deliberate, innovative and implacable leader with considerable administrative acumen and vast experience in his area of responsibility.

Commanding all French units – army as well as naval – along the French coast was 61-year-old **Vice-amiral Jean-Charles Abrial**, commonly known by his position: Amiral Nord. Born in Realmont, near Toulouse, Abrial entered the French Navy as a cadet in 1896. Noted for his successes hunting U-boats during World War I, afterwards he rose rather rapidly through the ranks, being promoted to *vice-amiral* in 1936 and commanding the 3e Région Maritime (the coastal defence area along France's Mediterranean shore) at Toulon through 1938. In December the next year he was appointed to the Forces Maritimes du Nord, which was headquartered at Dunkirk and responsible for the defence of the French Channel coast. While not as dynamic and far-sighted as Ramsay, Abrial was confident, aggressive and determined to 'hold on to Dunkirk till the last man and the last round'.

Abrial's subordinate land forces commander was **Général de corps d'armée M. B. Alfred Fagalde**. An infantry officer, Fagalde benefited well from his mastery of English, having seen considerable service in World War I as a liaison officer with the first BEF beginning in 1914 and by the end of the Great War was sent to London as the French military attaché. His experience with British troops and relationships with British officers made him appreciate that – especially at this stage in the defeat of France – complete alignment of aims was the only means of survival.

Originally a corps commander within Général d'armée Giraud's 7e Armée, Fagalde had advanced to the Scheldt Estuary in the opening days of the campaign, and when this army was disbanded, his 16e Corps d'armée was left holding the far north end of the Belgian line, between Antwerp and the sea, and was largely intact having seen little in the way of German attacks. On 24 May, Fagalde's corps was assigned to Vice-amiral Abrial's Forces Maritimes du Nord, giving him command of all French Army forces in the area. Upon learning that the BEF was falling back to Dunkirk, Fagalde was pleased that he would be working with Lord Gort.

General der Artillerie Georg von Küchler eventually commanded all German ground forces thrown against the Dunkirk perimeter. (IWM MH10679)

GERMAN COMMANDERS

In the end, the fate of the BEF, the French 1ère Armée and the Belgians would lie in the hands of two German officers: **General der Artillerie Georg von Küchler** and **Generalmajor Wolfram von Richthofen**. Küchler eventually was given command of the German ground forces attempting to eliminate the Allies ensconced in the Dunkirk Perimeter and Richthofen was charged with destroying them from the air.

Scion of a Junker family, Küchler was a Prussian Army officer through and through. Commissioned in 1901 as a *Leutnant* in the artillery, he had an excellent combat record throughout World War I and by 1918 was a member of the elite Großer Generalstab (Greater German General Staff – dissolved in the Treaty of Versailles). Continuing a steady rise under the Weimar Republic, by 1934 he commanded the 1. Infanterie-Division in East Prussia. Two years later, as a *Generalleutnant* and Inspector General of the service academies, he caught Hitler's eye and in turn became an ardent supporter. Against Poland, he led AOK 3 – advancing out of East Prussia as part of Bock's Heeresgruppe Nord (see Campaign 107: *Poland 1939* by Steven J. Zaloga, Osprey Publishing Ltd: Oxford, 2002) and was awarded the Ritterkreuz (Knight's Cross) for his successes. A highly professional officer – if somewhat unkempt – he was an effective leader and efficient administrator who, especially with his combat experience and thorough knowledge in the employment of artillery supporting infantry, was the best choice for finally smashing the fortified perimeter of the Dunkirk beachhead.

Generalmajor Wolfram von Richthofen. Generalfeldmarschall Erich von Manstein said Richthofen was 'the most outstanding air force leader we had in World War II'. (IWM HU55040)

According to Göring's boasts it would never come to that, for the insolent and impudent British and French forces 'trapped' at Dunkirk were to be obliterated by the fearsome Stuka dive-bombers of Wolfram von Richthofen's VIII Fliegerkorps. Cousin of the famous 'Red Baron' ace of World War I, Richthofen began his military career as a cavalry officer, seeing action on both fronts before transferring to the Imperial German air service. Becoming a fighter pilot in March 1918, he served in Jasta 11 (his cousin's unit) under Göring, scoring eight aerial victories. After the war he earned a degree in aeronautical engineering from the Technical University of Hanover and a PhD from the University of Berlin. By the time Göring brought the embryonic Luftwaffe into the open, von Richthofen was an *Oberst* in the Technical Bureau and in 1936 he went to Spain with the Condor Legion rising from chief of staff to commander in two years. Returning to Germany in May 1939 as a *Generalmajor* he had perfected the use of air power in coordinated, close support of ground troops in the attack.

Given command of a 'special-purpose air division' in which most of the Luftwaffe's Stuka *Gruppen* were concentrated, Richthofen supported the Panzers overrunning Poland in September and, towards the end of that month, was responsible for the near destruction of Warsaw from the air. Later designated VIII Fliegerkorps, his was a mobile and flexible command and in *Fall Gelb* (*Case Yellow*, the plan for the invasion of France and the Low Countries) Richthofen used it handily in first supporting Reichenau's AOK 6 penetration into Belgium before shifting south to support Guderian's crossing of the Meuse at Sedan and then providing 'flying artillery' for the Panzer columns charging across Picardy. Awarded the Ritterkreuz on 23 May, he returned to his HQ to begin planning strikes against the Allied defenders at Boulogne and Calais, French forces at Lille and their counterattacks at Amiens, and – eventually – against Dunkirk itself.

OPPOSING FORCES

I must not conceal from you that a great part of the BEF and its equipment will inevitably be lost.
BEF Commander Lord Gort to Secretary of State for War Anthony Eden, 26 May 1940

ALLIED FORCES

The British

By 10 May 1940, the British had deployed 13 infantry divisions (three of them for line-of-communications (LOC) duties and half the rest reservist Territorial Army units) and a tank brigade to France as the BEF. On that date nine of these had advanced in a front three divisions wide to take up positions along 27km (17 miles) of the Dyle River from Louvain to Wavre. After rebuffing the German IV and XI AK of Reichenau's AOK 6, the British were shocked to learn of the German breakthroughs at Sedan and Dinant and the need to fall back to the Escaut and later the Lys River.

After over two weeks of fighting and retreating, on 26 May, the once-mighty Allied armies in Flanders had been hammered into a rough boot-shaped pocket. The back of the boot conformed to the coastline from Zeebrugge to Gravelines and the front was formed by the Lys River as far as Menin. Except for the top end of this line held by part of Fagalde's 16e Corps d'armée, this 90km (56-mile) front was manned by the beleaguered Belgian Army. The 67km-long (42-mile) instep was held by a portion of the BEF – four divisions (1st, 3rd, 4th and 42nd) with two more (5th and 50th) being sent to backstop the flagging Belgian right flank – as far south as Bourghelles (on the French–Belgian border). The French 1ère Armée manned the swollen toe of the boot, their lines looping south along the river Sensée to end on the Haute Deule Canal north of Douai. The sole of the boot followed the chain of canals from Douai to Gravelines, ostensibly covered by four British divisions (2nd, 44th, 46th and 48th) with the northern end – from Gravelines through Watten – being held by the rest of Fagalde's 16e Corps d'armée.

Thus the BEF found itself – instead of being a homogeneous whole as it had been on the Dyle – split into two parts on opposite sides of the 25–40km-wide Dunkirk–Lille Pocket that extended some 112km (70 miles) from the coast. While the east side of the pocket seemed most threatened because of the rent being torn in the Belgian line around Courtrai, on the west side six Panzer divisions had driven to the sea and wheeled in echelon to rumble noisily up to all points along the Canal Line. Because III Corps could not hope to cover the front's 72km length, its four divisions were broken up into their individual battalions and scattered to hold bridges and small villages as strongpoints – or 'stops' as Lord Gort called them – thus forming a dotted line from La Bassée to Bergues. Consequently the western side of the pocket was open to exploitation by mobile armoured forces.

A convoy of lorries loaded with troops make their way through a Belgian town during their retreat from the Dyle Line. Unlike most French formations, the units of the BEF were largely motorized allowing for battlefield movements that were faster than both their German adversaries and their French allies. (IWM F4396)

15

Marching unceasingly, the French *poilus* of the 1ère Armée were exhausted, hungry and increasingly demoralized, yet they maintained their discipline and their determination to fight to the best of their ability and the last of their ammunition. (IWM F4315)

The French

Meanwhile at the 'bottom of the pocket' were the three corps of the French 1ère Armée. Having fought continuously for almost two weeks, Gén. Blanchard's 12 divisions (including three badly depleted armoured units) were on the brink of exhaustion. Because of the dislocation caused by the withdrawal from Belgium and punishing Luftwaffe air attacks on the French railway network, no supplies had reached them since 20 May. Quartermasters had been forced to forage food from the surrounding towns to feed the troops and supplies of artillery ammunition were virtually exhausted.

While the 1ère Armée was attempting a fighting withdrawal to the north along with the BEF, the primary French contribution to the defence of the Dunkirk beachhead was Gén. Fagalde's 16e Corps d'armée. Having lost half of one division (21e Division d'infanterie) on a tragic deployment towards Boulogne, this corps consisted of two intact infantry divisions and a horse-mounted reconnaissance battalion (18e Groupe de reconnaissance de corps d'armée, GRCA). On 23 May Fagalde was ordered to move his HQ and one division (68e Division d'infanterie) to the west between Gravelines and Saint-Omer, leaving the other (60e Division d'infanterie) with the Belgians to protect the Bruges (now Brugge) area.

Informed he was to command all French ground forces along the Channel coast, Fagalde immediately went to Dunkirk to confer with Vice-amiral Abrial and assess what other units he had to work with. Manning the area's fixed defences were the three reserve battalions of the 272e Demi-brigade d'infanterie assigned to the 11,000-man Secteur fortifié de Flandres under Général de brigade Eugène Barthélemy, headquartered in the ancient walled and moated city of Bergues, 8.5km (5 miles) south of Dunkirk. Additionally there were two training battalions, three labour battalions and five battalions from his decimated 21e Division d'infanterie (mainly the 137e RI) holding Gravelines and Bourbourg. For artillery Fagalde had six battalions of 75mm guns, five of 155mm guns and two of 25mm anti-tank guns.

Allied naval forces

Guarding the eastern approaches to the English Channel, Dover Command's mission was primarily centred on anti-submarine and mine warfare. Ramsay began the May campaign with 11 destroyers – mostly old, small World War I types – but in a wide variety of operations along the French, Belgian and Dutch coasts one was lost and two were so badly damaged they had to be withdrawn from operations. The survivors were supplemented by three old destroyers and two modern ones, plus a similar and contemporary British-built Polish example. In the shoal-ridden Channel and tight confines of French harbours, the destroyers' shallow draught and excellent manoeuvrability proved premium assets.

For mine warfare Ramsay originally had 30 minesweepers and 24 armed trawlers equipped for minesweeping. In the course of the campaign, the command would be reinforced with 20 additional destroyers, six newer minelaying destroyers and six fleet minesweepers.

Generally, Ramsay's 39 British destroyers were of two categories; more numerous were the 20–22-year-old boats of the V and W classes. Too old, small and lightly armed for Fleet duties these 1,188-ton warships were still very useful, especially for convoy and coastal duties.

Also available to Dover Command was the 1st Flotilla's newer, larger and more powerful 1,350-ton G-class boats and the 20th Flotilla's modified 1,400-ton E- and I-class minelaying destroyers. However, the Royal Navy had yet to acquire effective fast-firing anti-aircraft weapons, making both the newer large and the older small destroyers very vulnerable to air – especially dive-bomber – attacks.

Like Dover Command, Amiral Nord had a sizeable group of large and small destroyers based at Dunkirk to guard the French side of the English Channel. These initially included four large (2,126/2,440-ton) destroyers, nine (1,298/1,356-ton) destroyers and six small (669-ton) torpedo boats, augmented by seven small 'submarine chasers' and nine naval auxiliaries.

RAF Supermarine Spitfires on patrol. A match for the Messerschmitt Bf 109E, the elegantly designed and manoeuvrable British fighter received its first taste of combat over Dunkirk, its performance limited by the RAF's restrictive three-plane 'vic' formations, rigid attack tactics and the raw inexperience of the pilots. (IWM CH740)

Allied air forces

On 21 May the ragged remnant of the BEF's air component flew home to England. Similarly, once Groupe d'armées 1 was cut off in the north the Armée de l'Air's 25e Groupement of fighters (Groupes de Chasse III/1 and II/8, originally covering Giraud's 7e Armée) was withdrawn south of the Somme. That day French and British air commanders met to revise the arrangements for supporting the Allied armies in the north. Because the Armée de l'Air's Zone d'Operations Aériennes Nord (Northern Zone of Air Operations, ZOAN) had retired to the Paris region and the lower Seine it lacked any ability to protect Groupe d'armées 1. Thus, it was agreed that ZOAN, coupled with the British Advanced Air Striking Force (AASF), would cover the Somme and Aisne sectors while the UK-based 11 Group (fighters) and 2 Group (light bombers) supported the Allied armies trapped in the north.

In all, RAF Fighter Command had expended 386 Hurricanes and lost 56 pilots killed and 18 captured in the fighting in France. This left 11 Group with 269 serviceable day fighters (114 Spitfires, 137 Hurricanes and 18 Defiants) in 21 squadrons, five of which (flying Spitfires) were retained for home defence. Therefore 16 squadrons with a total strength of about 200 machines, would provide air cover over the Allied armies trapped in the Dunkirk Pocket.

Bombing support would be provided by 2 Group's Bristol Blenheim IV twin-engine light bombers. Having lost 60 of this type in 16 days of almost continuous combat operations, the Group's six squadrons were now down to 60 serviceable examples, manned by very tired aircrews.

A 10.5cm le FH 18 moves up during the advance across Belgium. Contrary to British propaganda at the time, subsequent histories and popular belief, most of the forces facing the BEF were not modern mechanized units but 1918-style infantry formations with horse-drawn artillery. (IWM HU3894)

GERMAN FORCES

After the BEF's small, but stinging, spoiling attack at Arras on the 21st, all of Guderian's superiors began worrying that the hard-charging Panzers had outstripped their infantry consorts to the point where they were now dreadfully exposed. His immediate superior – General der Kavallerie Ewald von Kleist – was worried about what the British counterattack portended and the rising tank losses being experienced in the last few days. About the same time (1640hrs on 23 May) Kleist's new boss – AOK 4 commander Generaloberst Günther Hans von Kluge – telephoned Heeresgruppe A commander, Generaloberst Gerd von Rundstedt, advising that 'the troops would welcome an opportunity to close up tomorrow'. Rundstedt, who had his own reservations about continuing the unbridled offensive and wanted a period of rest and regrouping before attacking south of the Somme, consented readily and at 2000hrs Kluge telephoned both *Panzergruppen* HQs stating that AOK 4 would not advance during the 24th in order to allow the infantry to close up with the Panzers.

That day Hitler visited Rundstedt's Heeresgruppe A HQ (a vine-encrusted townhouse in Charleville, France) and a discussion on the means to subsequently eliminate the Allied pocket ensued. Influenced by Generaloberst Wilhelm Keitel, the Chief of the Oberkommando der Wehrmacht (OKW), Hitler had become worried that the Panzers would be bogged down in Flanders and wanted to preserve them for the *coup de grâce* to be delivered against the French. Additionally, for political reasons he wanted Heeresgruppe B to push the Allied forces out of Belgium so that their final defeat would take place on French soil and not in neutral territory. Thus Hitler became even more adamant about stopping the Panzers than his generals.

Returning to Felsennest (his battle HQ, a hunting lodge in the forests at Münstereifel, south of Bonn) Hitler directed the OKH to issue a *Haltbefehl*, 'halt order'. As passed to Kluge's AOK 4 it read 'By the Führer's orders… hold [along] the favourable defensive line Lens–Béthune–Aire–Saint-Omer–Gravelines, and allow the enemy to attack it…. The principal thing now is to husband the armoured formations for later and more important tasks.'

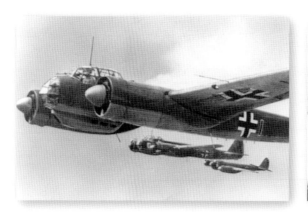

Thus the Allied forces trapped in the Dunkirk–Lille Pocket were caught between what the Germans called 'the hammer and the anvil'. To the east were the German infantry divisions of Bock's Heeresgruppe B, which consisted of two armies: Küchler's AOK 18, which had completed the conquest of Holland and deployed across the Scheldt to become Bock's right wing, and Reichenau's AOK 6. These were entirely slow-moving 1918-style infantry formations – 21 divisions in six corps – composed of foot soldiers and horse-drawn artillery. All of Bock's motorized and mechanized units – as well as all OKH reserves – had been sent around the Allied pocket to join Rundstedt's drive to the sea.

Halting along the Canal Line to the west were the Panzer units hot from their headlong dash to the Channel. Facing the Allied pocket, Kluge's AOK 4 controlled Panzergruppe Kleist (minus XIV AK (mot.) protecting the south flank) and the newly created Panzergruppe Hoth, formerly XV AK (mot.) now joined by the XVI and XXXIX AK (mot.) from Heeresgruppe B. Three infantry corps supported them. All told, Heeresgruppe A had swelled to 71 divisions in 22 corps, but most of these were in AOK 12 and 16, which had been left behind to control the flow of infantry marching into the extended German salient and protect the south flank along the Somme.

Just as worrisome as the lack of infantry support was the fact that the Panzer units had become badly depleted in their combats with Allied defenders and in their drive across northern France. Out of 2,428 tanks with which Kleist had begun the campaign (see Battle Orders 32: *Panzer Divisions: The Blitzkrieg Years 1939–40* by Pier Paolo Battistelli, Osprey Publishing Ltd: Oxford, 2007), he estimated 30 per cent had been lost in combat or were irreparably damaged. Another 20 per cent had been left behind because of mechanical breakdowns or were in need of repair before continuing across the Aa. This left him with only 1,220 operational tanks but with the respite provided by the 'stop order', it was estimated that the 730 reparable vehicles could be back in their units in three days or less.

The Luftwaffe

The Luftwaffe too had suffered heavy losses during the opening stages of *Fall Gelb*. While they had driven the BEF's air component from the Continent and reduced the Armée de l'Air to impotence, heavy attrition had eroded the German air force's strength; 641 combat aircraft (as of 25 May) were lost (23 per cent of its starting inventory) and serviceability was down to 50 per cent. Even with timely replacements General der Flieger Albrecht Kesselring, commanding Luftflotte 2, reported that many bomber *Gruppen* (groups) were reduced to 15 serviceable aircraft (against a statutory strength of 36).

Nevertheless, on 24 May, when the Nazi leaders began to debate how to conclude the dramatically successful western offensive, Göring begged Hitler for a chance at glory, saying 'Mein Führer, leave the destruction of the enemy surrounded at Dunkirk to me and my Luftwaffe.' Before the day ended Hitler granted Göring's request in OKW War Directive No. 13, ordering the Luftwaffe 'to break down all resistance of the surrounded enemy forces, to prevent the escape of the British forces across the Channel, and to secure the southern flank of Heeresgruppe A.'

This was easier said than done. Because the Heinkels and Dorniers were operating at the limits of their range – I and II Fliegerkorps were still largely based in Germany, some as far as 480km (300 miles) from Dunkirk – they were restricted to a single mission each day. General der Flieger Alfred Keller's Holland-based IV Fliegerkorps was closer but was needed to support AOK 18's assault on the Belgians and Generalleutnant Ritter von Greim's V Fliegerkorps was increasingly tasked with protecting Rundstedt's southern flank by striking the Allied forces marshalling south of the Somme. This left Richthofen's VIII Fliegerkorps as the only air command capable of executing Göring's stated intention, but even they had problems.

VIII Fliegerkorps' two Junkers 87 Stuka dive-bomber *Geschwader* ('wings' – Stukageschwader 2 and 77) tried to follow closely behind their armoured charges, but they just could not keep up. On 24 May Stukas of Stukageschwader 2 leapfrogged to Guise, near Saint-Quentin, 170km (106 miles) from Dunkirk, while Stukageschwader 77 remained at Rocroi another 70km (43 miles) to the rear, operating at the very limits of their combat radius.

The Kriegsmarine

With the German Navy's heavy surface units crippled in the ongoing Norwegian campaign and the Channel too narrow, shallow and heavily mined for large-scale U-boat operations, the Kriegsmarine was limited to using its high-speed torpedo boats or *Schnellboote* (or *S-boote*, called 'E-boats', short for 'enemy boats', by the British) for hit-and-run attacks, normally at night.

Marinegruppe Kommando West, Admiral Alfred Saalwächter, had two flotillas (totalling nine) of these fast light attack craft and they moved to the main Dutch naval base at Den Helder soon after its capture. Supported by two tenders and staging from the Dutch naval base at Vlissingen (Flushing), they soon proved their worth, *S.21* and *S.23* sinking the large French destroyer *Jaguar* as it approached Dunkirk on 22/23 May, and *S.34* sinking the 694-ton coastal freighter *Aboukir* near the North Hinder buoy six nights later.

Supplementing the S-boats was a single flotilla of seven small 291-ton (341-ton submerged) Type IIC and two smaller Type IIB coastal/training U-boats. Having lost three U-boats in October 1939 to mines in the Channel, the Kriegsmarine was quite naturally reluctant to send their submarines into the shallow, shoal-ridden waters but they did station four of these small boats in what the Germans called the 'Hoofen', the south-eastern corner of the North Sea between the Kent coastline and the Scheldt Estuary.

ORDERS OF BATTLE

(As of 30 May 1940, except when noted)

ALLIED FORCES TRAPPED IN THE DUNKIRK–LILLE POCKET

BRITISH EXPEDITIONARY FORCE – GENERAL LORD GORT

GHQ Troops
1st Army Tank Brigade – Brigadier Charles Norman
    4th/7th Battalion The Royal Tank Regiment
Not brigaded:
    12th Battalion The Royal Lancers
    13th/18th Battalion The King's Royal Hussars
    1st Battalion The Welsh Guards
    1st Battalion The Lothians and Border Yeomanry
    9th Battalion The West Yorkshire Regiment
Machine-gun units
    7th Battalion The Cheshire Regiment
    1st/8th Battalion The Middlesex Regiment
    4th Battalion The Gordon Highlanders
    6th Battalion The Argyll and Sutherland Highlanders
Pioneer units
    6th, 7th, 8th and 9th Battalions The King's Own Royal Regiment
    6th Battalion The Royal Scots Fusiliers
    7th Battalion The Royal Norfolk Regiment
    1st/6th Battalion The South Staffordshire Regiment
Artillery
    1st and 2nd Regiments RHA
    32nd, 98th, 115th and 139th Field Regiments RA
    1st, 2nd, 4th, 58th, 61st, 63rd, 65th and 69th Medium Regiments RA
    1st, 51st and 52nd Heavy Regiments RA
    1st, 2nd and 3rd Super Heavy Regiments RA
Anti-aircraft units
    1st, 4th, 6th, 69th and 85th Anti-Aircraft Regiments RA
    1st, 51st and 58th Light Anti-Aircraft Regiments RA
    1st, 2nd and 3rd Searchlight Regiments RA

I Corps – Lt. Gen. Michael G. H. Barker
1st Division – Maj. Gen. The Hon. Harold R. L. G. Alexander
    1st Guards Brigade
    2nd Brigade
    3rd Brigade
    2nd, 19th and 67th Field Regiments RA
    21st Anti-Tank Regiment
42nd (East Lancashire) Division – Maj. Gen. William Holmes
    125th Brigade
    126th Brigade
    127th Brigade
    52nd and 53rd Field Regiments RA
    56th Anti-Tank Regiment RA
Corps troops:
    Machine-gun units
        2nd and 4th Battalions The Cheshire Regiment
        2nd Battalion The Manchester Regiment
    Artillery
        27th and 140th Field Regiments RA
        3rd and 5th Medium Regiments RA
        52nd Light Anti-Aircraft Regiment RA

II Corps – Lt. Gen. Alan F. Brooke
3rd Division – Maj. Gen. Bernard L. Montgomery
    7th Guards Brigade
    8th Brigade
    9th Brigade
    7th, 33rd and 76th Field Regiments RA
    20th Anti-Tank Regiment RA
4th Division – Maj. Gen. Dudley Johnson
    10th Brigade
    11th Brigade
    12th Brigade
    22nd, 30th and 77th Field Regiments RA
    14th Anti-Tank Regiment RA
5th Division – Maj. Gen. Harold E. Franklyn
    13th Brigade
    (15th Brigade deployed to Norway)
    17th Brigade
    143rd Brigade (detached from 48th Division)
    9th, 91st and 92nd Field Regiments RA
    52nd Anti-Tank Regiment RA
50th Division (Northumbrian) – Maj. Gen. Giffard le Q. Martel
    150th Brigade
    151st Brigade
    4th Battalion The Royal Northumberland Fusiliers
    72nd and 74th Field Regiments RA
    65th Anti-Tank Regiment RA
Corps troops:
    Artillery
        60th and 88th Army Field Regiments RA
        53rd and 59th Medium Regiments RA
        53rd Light Anti-Aircraft Regiment RA
        2nd Survey Regiment RA
    Machine-gun units
        2nd and 1st/7th Battalions The Middlesex Regiment
        2nd Battalion The Royal Northumberland Fusiliers

III Corps – Maj. Gen. S. R. Wason
2nd Division – Maj. Gen. Noel Irwin
    4th Brigade – destroyed at Béthune and La Paradis, 27 May
    5th Brigade – largely destroyed at La Bassée, 27 May
    6th Brigade – destroyed at Robecq and Saint-Venant, 27 May
    25th Brigade – detached from 50th Division
    10th, 16th and 99th Field Regiments RA
    13th Anti-Tank Regiment RA
    2nd Light Armoured Reconnaissance Brigade
44th (Home Counties) Division – Maj. Gen. Edmund A. Osborne
    131st Brigade
    132nd Brigade
    133rd Brigade
    57th, 58th and 65th Field Regiments RA
    57th Anti-Tank Regiment RA
    1st Light Armoured Reconnaissance Brigade
46th (North Midland and West Riding) Division – Maj. Gen. Harry Curtis
    137th Brigade (2nd/5th Battalion The West Yorkshire Regiment only)
    138th Brigade – nearly destroyed at Abbeville 20 May
    139th Brigade
48th (South Midland) Division – Maj. Gen. Andrew F. A. N. Thorne
    144th Brigade
    145th Brigade – surrendered near Watou on 29 May
    18th, 24th and 68th Field Regiments RA
    53rd Anti-Tank Regiment RA

Corps troops:
    Artillery
        5th Regiment RHA
        97th Field Regiment RA
        51st and 56th Medium Regiments RA
        54th Light Anti-Aircraft Regiment RA
        3rd Survey Regiment RA
    Machine-gun units
        7th Battalion The Royal Northumberland Fusiliers
        1st/9th Battalion The Manchester Regiment
        1st Battalion Princess Louise's Kensington Regiment

Line of communications troops*
12th (Eastern) Division – Maj. Gen. R. L. Petre
    35th Brigade – destroyed at Abbeville, 20 May
    36th Brigade – destroyed at Doullens, 20 May
    37th Brigade – largely destroyed at Amiens, 20 May,
        remnants retired south of the Somme River
23rd (Northumbrian) Division (-) – Maj. Gen. William Herbert
    69th Brigade – badly battered on the Scarpe, 20 May;
        escaped to Dunkirk
    70th Brigade – destroyed at Blairville-Mercatel, 20 May
*51st Division attached to French 3e Armée

ROYAL NAVY (as of 26 May 1940)

Flag Officer Dover – V. Adm. Bertram Home Ramsey
Captain (Destroyers) 19th Destroyer Flotilla 11 older destroyers
Detached from 1st Destroyer Flotilla   two modern
    destroyers plus one Polish
1st and 2nd Anti-Submarine Striking Force six patrol sloops
    (coastal corvettes)
1st Motor Torpedo Boat Flotilla   six motor torpedo boats
4th Minesweeper Flotilla   five minesweepers
5th Minesweeper Flotilla   eight minesweepers
6th Minesweeper Flotilla   three minesweepers
7th Minesweeper Flotilla   five minesweepers
8th Minesweeper Flotilla   three minesweepers
10th Minesweeper Flotilla   six minesweepers
Minesweeping Group 51   nine minesweeping trawlers
Minesweeping Group 61   nine minesweeping trawlers
10th Anti-Submarine Striking Force   six trawlers
11th Anti-Submarine Striking Force   six trawlers
21st Anti-Submarine Group   six trawlers
40th Anti-Submarine Group   six trawlers

Reinforcing units
Anti-aircraft Cruiser HMS *Calcutta* from the Nore Command
1st Destroyer Flotilla three destroyers from the Nore Command
5th Destroyer Flotilla two destroyers from the Nore Command
9th Destroyer Flotilla two destroyers from Western Approaches
    Command
11th Destroyer Flotilla   five destroyers from Western
    Approaches Command
15th Destroyer Flotilla   one destroyer from Western
    Approaches Command
16th Destroyer Flotilla   four destroyers from
    Portsmouth Command
17th Destroyer Flotilla   two destroyers from Western
    Approaches Command
18th Destroyer Flotilla   one destroyer from Western
    Approaches Command
20th Destroyer Flotilla   six minelaying destroyers from
    the Nore Command
1st Sloop Division   one escort sloop from Western
    Approaches Command

1st Minesweeping Flotilla   two minesweepers from Scapa
    Flow
12th Minesweeper Flotilla   four minesweepers from
    Harwich
Thames Estuary Defence Flotilla two gunboats from the Nore
    Command
1st Motor Anti-Submarine Boat Flotilla   seven motor anti-
    submarine boats
Three paddle anti-aircraft ships
three armed boarding vessels
42 personnel ships
Eight hospital carriers
Three store ships
13 army landing craft
Six RAF seaplane tender boats
One Belgian Navy patrol boat
Five Belgian tugs
43 Belgian trawlers
Four Belgian passenger launches
One Royal Netherlands Navy motorboat
40 Dutch *schuyts* (with RN crews)
One Dutch yacht
25 yachts
40 tugs
61 drifters
346 assorted small craft

ROYAL AIR FORCE

Fighter Command – Air Chief Marshal Sir Hugh Dowding
11 Group – Air Vice-Marshal Keith Park
    No. 17 Sqn., 13 Hurricanes, Kenley
    No. 19 Sqn., 13 Spitfires, Hornchurch
    No. 32 Sqn., four Hurricanes, Biggin Hill
    No. 41 Sqn., 17 Spitfires, Hornchurch
    No. 56 Sqn., 16 Hurricanes, North Weald
    No. 64 Sqn., 13 Spitfires, Kenley
    No. 65 Sqn., 1 Spitfire, Hornchurch
    No. 79 Sqn., 6 Hurricanes, Biggin Hill
    No. 92 Sqn., 13 Spitfires, Northolt
    No. 111 Sqn., 17 Hurricanes, North Weald
    No. 145 Sqn., 18 Hurricanes, Tangmere
    No. 151 Sqn., 19 Hurricanes, North Weald
    No. 213 Sqn., 10 Hurricanes, Biggin Hill
    No. 222 Sqn., 15 Spitfires, Hornchurch
    No. 229 Sqn., eight Hurricanes, Biggin Hill
    No. 235 Sqn., Blenheim IFs, Bircham Newton
    No. 242 Sqn., 11 Hurricanes, Biggin Hill
    No. 245 Sqn., NA Hurricanes, Hawkinge
    No. 264 Sqn., 15 Defiants, Duxford
    No. 601 Sqn., 15 Hurricanes, Tangmere
    No. 609 Sqn., 18 Spitfires, Northolt
    No. 610 Sqn., 12 Spitfires, Biggin Hill
    No. 616 Sqn., 12 Spitfires, Hornchurch

Bomber Command
2 Group
    No. 15 Sqn., Blenheim IVs, Wyton
    No. 21 Sqn., Blenheim IVs, Wattisham
    No. 40 Sqn., Blenheim IVs, Wyton
    No. 82 Sqn., Blenheim IVs, Wattisham
    No. 107 Sqn., Blenheim IVs, Wattisham
    No. 110 Sqn., Blenheim IVs, Wattisham

Coastal Command
16 Group
    No. 48 Sqn., Ansons, Thorney Island
    No. 206 Sqn., Hudsons, Bircham Newton
    No. 220 Sqn., Hudsons, Thornaby
    No. 254 Sqn., Blenheim IVs, Detling
    No. 500 Sqn., Ansons, Detling

Attached Fleet Air Arm squadrons
    NAS 801, Skuas, Detling
    NAS 806, Skuas, Manston
    NAS 815, Swordfish, Detling
    NAS 825, Swordfish, Detling
    NAS 826, Albacores, Ford

FRENCH ARMY

Groupe d'armées 1 – Gén. d'armée Jean Georges Maurice
  Blanchard
1ère Armée – Gén. de corps René Jacques Adolphe Prioux
3e Corps d'armée – Gén. de corps Fournelle de la Laurencie
  1ère Division d'infanterie motorisée – surrendered at Lille,
  31 May 1940
    7e GRDI
  2e Division d'infanterie Nord-Africaine – surrendered at
  Lille, 31 May 1940
    92e GRDI
  12e Division d'infanterie motorisée – Gén. de brig.
  Louis Janssen
    8e RZ
    150e RI
    25e RAD
    225e RAD
    3e GRDI
  Remnant of 32e Division d'infanterie – Gén. Maurice Lucas
    III/122e RI
    III/143e RI
4e Corps d'armée – Gén. de corps Aymer – surrendered at Lille,
  31 May 1940
  15e Division d'infanterie motorisée
  1ère Division d'infanterie Marocaine
  4e Division d'infanterie
  7e GRCA
  106e RALH
  604e RP
5e Corps d'armée (motorisée) – Gén. de corps René Altmayer –
  surrendered at Lille, 31 May 1940
  25e Division d'infanterie motorisée
  5e Division d'infanterie Nord-Africaine
  104e RALT
  605e RP
Corps de cavalerie – badly depleted in continuous combat
  1ère Division légère mécanique – Gén. de brig. Picard
    4e RC
    6e RC
    18e RD
    4e RDP
    74e RATT
  2e Division légère mécanique – Gén. de brig. Bougrain
    8e RC
    13e RD
    29e RD
    1re RDP
    71e RATTT

  3e Division légère Mécanique – Gén. de div. Langlois
    1re RC
    2e RC
    12e RC
    11e RDP
    76e RATT
  3e GRCA (motorisée)

Formerly of 7e Armée – Reassigned to Forces Maritimes du Nord
  on 24 May 1940
16e Corps d'armée – Gén. de corps M. B. Alfred Fagalde
  21e Division d'infanterie – Gén. de brig. Félix Lanquetot
    48e RI – largely destroyed near Boulogne on 22 May
    65e RI – largely destroyed near Calais on 22 May
    137e RI
    35e RAD
    255e RAD
    27e GRDI
  60e Division d'infanterie – Gén. de brig. Deslaurens
    241e RI
    270e RI – largely destroyed during retreat between
  Zeebrugge and Nieuport on 29 May
    271e RI
    50e RA – attached to Belgian Army, lost on 28 May
    II/307e RAD
    68e GRDI
  68e Division d'infanterie – Gén. de div. Beaufrère
    224e RI
    225e RI
    341e RI
    89e RAD
    289e RAD
    I/307e RAD
    59e GRDI
  115e RALH
  407e RP (from 7e Armée)
  616e RP
  18e GRCA
Secteur fortifié de Flandres – Gén. de brig. Eugène Barthélemy
  272e Demi-brigade d'infanterie – Lt. Col. Lemistre
    14e RRT (one battalion only)
    15e RRT (one battalion only)
    221e RRT (one battalion only)
    161e RAP
  Groupe des Secteurs Nord (autonomous coastal defence
  fortress units)
    IV/310e RI – Dunkirk
    V/310e RI – Calais
    VI/310e RI – Boulogne
    VII/310e RI – Gravelines
  21e Centre d'instruction divisionnaire
    21e Bn./110e RI
    21e Bn./129e RI
    147e Bataillon de Sapeurs-Mineurs

FRENCH NAVY

Forces Maritimes du Nord – Vice-amiral Jean-Charles Abrial
'Pas de Calais' Flotilla – Contre-amiral Marcel Landriau
    Two large torpedo boat destroyers
    Six torpedo boat destroyers
    Six torpedo boats
    Five dispatch boats (sloops)
    Two minesweepers
    Six submarine chasers
    Three personnel ships (detached to RN)

Additional Ships
12 motor torpedo boats
13 auxiliary minesweepers
7 auxiliary patrol vessels
Six troop transports
12 cargo ships
59 trawlers

GERMAN FORCES

GERMAN ARMY

Heeresgruppe A – Gen.Obst. Gerd von Rundstedt
AOK 4 – Gen.Obst. Günther Hans von Kluge
Panzergruppe Kleist – Gen. Ewald von Kleist
    XIV AK (mot.) – Gen. Gustav von Wietersheim
        AR (mot) 782
        9. Panzer-Division – Gen.Lt. Dr Albert Ritter von Hubicki
        – from Heeresgruppe B/AOK 18/XXXIX AK
            PR 33 (-)
            SR (mot.) 10 (-)
            SR (mot.) 11 (-)
            AR (mot.) 102 (-)
            AR 9
            PzJäg.-Abt. (mot.) 50
            Pion.-Bat. 86
            Nachr.-Abt. 85
        20. Infanterie-Division (mot.) – Gen.Lt. Mauriz Wiktorin
    zu Hainburg – from Heeresgruppe B/AOK 6/XVI AK
            IR (mot.) 76
            IR (mot.) 80
            AR (mot.) 20 (-)
            I./AR (mot.) 58
            Aufkl.-Abt. 20
            Beob.-Abt. 20
            Pzab.-Abt. (mot.) 20
            Pion.-Bat. 20
            Nachr.-Abt. 20
            Attached: IR (mot.) 'Grossdeutschland'
            IR (mot.) 'Leibstandarte SS Adolf Hitler'
         11. Schützenbrigade (mot.) – Obst. Angern – from
    Höheres Kommando XXXI/Denmark
            IR (mot.) 110
            IR (mot.) 111
            MG.-Bat. (mot.) 13
            III./AR (mot) 677

Heeresgruppe B – Gen.Obst. Fedor von Bock
AOK 6 – Gen.Obst. Walter von Reichenau
    X AK – Gen.Lt. Christian Hansen (from AOK 18)
        14. Infanterie-Division – Gen.Lt. Peter Wyer
            IR 11
            IR 53
            IR 101
            AR 74 (+)
            Aufkl.-Abt. 14
            PzJäg.-Abt. 14
            Pion.-Bat. 14
            Nachr.-Abt. 14
        18. Infanterie-Division – Gen.Lt. Friedrich-Carl Cranz
            IR 30
            IR 51
            IR 54
            AR 18 (+)

            Aufkl.-Abt. 18
            Pzab.-Abt. (mot.) 18
            Pion.-Bat. 18
            Nachr.-Abt. 18
        254. Infanterie-Division – Gen.Lt. Walter Behschnitt
            IR 454
            IR 474
            IR 484
            AR 254
            Aufkl.-Abt. 254
            Pzab.-Abt. 254
            Pion.-Bat. 254
            Nachr.-Abt. 254

AOK 18 – Gen. Georg von Küchler
    IX AK – Gen. Hermann Geyer (from AOK 6)
        AR (mot) 617
        56. Infanterie-Division – Gen.Lt. Karl Kriebel
            IR 171
            IR 192
            IR 234
            AR 156
            Aufkl.-Abt. 156
            PzJäg.-Abt. 156
            Pion.-Bat. 156
            Nachr.-Abt. 156
        216. Infanterie-Division – Gen.Lt. Hermann Böttcher
            IR 348
            IR 396
            IR 398
            AR 216
            Aufkl.-Abt. 216
            Pzab.-Abt. 216
            Pion.-Bat. 216
            Nachr.-Abt. 216
    XXVI AK – Gen.Lt. Albert Wodrig
        AR (mot.) 785
         208. Infanterie-Division – Gen.Maj. Moritz Andreas – to
    IX AK as of 2 June 1940
            IR 309
            IR 337
            IR 338
            AR 208
            Aufkl.-Abt. 208
            PzJäg.-Abt. 208
            Pion.-Bat. 208
            Nachr.-Abt. 208
        256. Infanterie-Division – Gen.Lt. Gerhard Kauffmann
            IR 456
            IR 476
            IR 481
            AR 256
            Aufkl.-Abt. 256
            PzJäg.-Abt. 256
            Pion.-Bat. 256
            Nachr.-Abt. 256

LUFTWAFFE – GENERALFELDMARSHALL HERMAN GÖRING

Luftflotte 2 – Gen. Albrecht Kesselring
(Fern)/Aufklärungsgruppe 122
Wekusta 26

I Fliegerkorps– Gen. Ulrich Grauert
  5. (Fern)/Aufklärungsgruppe 122
  KG 1, He 111H
  KG 76, Do 17Z
  KG 77, Do 17Z
  JG 77 (-), Bf 109E
  I.(J)/LG 2 , Bf 109E
  II.(J)/Trägergrp. 186, Bf 109E
  ZG 76 (-), Bf 110C
IV Fliegerkorps – Gen. Alfred Keller
  1. (Fern)/Aufklärungsgruppe 121
  LG 1, He 111H
  KG 4, He 111P
  KG 27, He 111P
  KG 54, He 111P
  I./KG 30, Ju 88A
Jagdfliegerführer 2 – Gen.Lt. Hans von Döring
  JG 26 (+), Bf 109E
  JG 51 (+), Bf 109E

Luftflotte 3 – Gen. der Flieger Hugo Sperrle
(Fern)/Aufklärungsgruppe 123 (-)
Wekusta 51
II Fliegerkorps– Gen. Bruno Lörzer
  3. (Fern)/Aufklärungsgr.121
  KG 2, Do 17Z
  KG 3, Do 17Z
  KG 53, He 111H
VIII Fliegerkorps– Gen.Maj. Wolfram von Richthofen
  2.(Fern)/Aufklärungsgr.123
  StG 1 (-), Ju 87B

StG 2, Ju 87B
StG 77, Ju 87B
IV.(St)/LG 1, Ju 87B
I.(St)/Trägergrp. 186, Ju 87B
JG 2, Bf 109E
JG 27, Bf 109E
Jagdfliegerführer 3 – Obst. Gerd von Massow
  JG 52 (-), Bf 109E
  JG 53, Bf 109E
  JG 54, Bf 109E
  ZG 2, Bf 110C
  ZG 26 (+), Bf 110C

KRIEGSMARINE – GROSSADMIRAL ERICH RAEDER

Marinegruppe Kommando West – Adm. Alfred Saalwächter
Küstenbefehlshaber Südwest (Den Helder) – V.Adm. Lothar von
  Arnauld
  1. Schnellbootsflotilla – Klt. Heinz Birnbacher
    Four S-boats
    Tender *Tsingtau*
  2. Schnellbootsflotilla – Klt. Rudolf Petersen
    Five S-boats
    Tender *Tanga*
Unterseebootsführung – KsZ. Eberhard Godt
  1. Unterseebootsflotilla – Korvettenkapitän Hans
  Eckermann
    Nine Type II coastal submarines
    Tender *Saar*

ABBREVIATIONS

AK –	Armeekorps
AR –	Artillerie-Regiment
Aufkl.-Abt. –	Aufklarüngs-Abteilung
Beob.-Abt. –	Beobachtungs-Abteiling
GRCA –	Groupe de reconnaissance de corps d'armée
GRDI –	Groupe de reconnaissance de division d'infanterie
JG –	Jagdgeschwader
KG –	Kampfgeschwader
LG –	Lehrgeschwader
MG.-Bat. –	Maschinengewehr-Bataillon
Nachr.-Abt. –	Nachrichten-Abteilung
Pion.-Bat. –	Pionier-Abteilung
PR –	Panzer-Regiment
Pzab.-Abt. –	Panzerabwehr Abteilung
PzJäg.-Abt –	Panzerjäger-Abteilung
RAD –	Régiment d'artillery divisionnaire
RALH –	Régiment d'artillerie lourde hippomobile
RALT –	Régiment d'artillerie lourde tractée
RAP –	Régiment d'artillerie de position
RATTT –	Régiment d'artillery divisionnaire tractée tous-terrains
RC –	Régiment de cuirassiers
RD –	Régiment de dragons
RDP –	Régiment de dragons portés
RI –	Régiment d'infanterie
RP –	Régiment de pionniers
RRT –	Régiment régionaux de travailleurs
RZ –	Régiment de zouaves
SR –	Schützen-Regiment
StG –	Stukageschwader
ZG –	Zerstörergeschwader

OPPOSING PLANS

You are now authorized to operate towards the coast forthwith in conjunction with the French and Belgian armies.
Secretary of State for War Anthony Eden to BEF Commander Lord Gort, just before 1900hrs, 26 May 1940

OPERATION *DYNAMO*

The ability to rescue the BEF actually depended on two plans that met at the water's edge. The BEF had to organize a withdrawal into and defence of the Dunkirk perimeter, as well as develop an embarkation programme; Dover Command had to organize, control and protect the shipping, its routes and the embarkation points. To prevent the Luftwaffe from interrupting the desperate process, the RAF had to provide continuous, effective air cover.

To orchestrate the BEF's part, Lord Gort chose III Corps commander Lieutenant-General Sir Ronald Adam. His primary staff elements consisted of the BEF's quartermaster-general, chief engineer, and Lt. Col. Bridgeman. Adam was charged with surveying the ground and making all necessary plans for a defensive perimeter, organizing the means to sustain the 250,000 British troops, and making the preparations for effective and timely embarkations.

To establish a defensible perimeter, Lord Gort sent the commander of the 48th (South Midland) Division, Major-General Andrew F. A. N. Thorne, his staff and his 144th Brigade to Dunkirk on 25 May. Upon arrival, Thorne found that Gén. Fagalde had already established a strong defence in depth, with what remained of 21e Division d'infanterie deployed behind the line Gravelines–Watten–Cassel and Général de division Beaufrère's 68e Division d'infanterie entrenched along a secondary line of canals connecting Mardyck–Spycker–Bergues, heavily supported by artillery. Consequently Thorne placed the 144th Brigade on the left flank of the secondary line at Wormhoudt.

Working together, Adam and Fagalde quickly mapped out a defensible 48km (30-mile) perimeter using as many contiguous water barriers as possible. With Fagalde already holding the west side of the perimeter, it was naturally agreed that arriving French troops would be placed west of the Dunkirk–Bergues Canal. In the British portion Adam placed II Corps furthest east, covering the two canals forming the corner at Nieuport and extending almost to Furnes. I Corps would defend the centre around Furnes and III Corps would fill in between there and Bergues.

Adam planned for the BEF to be evacuated in reverse order: III, II and I Corps with the last providing the rearguard. Embarkation assembly areas and control centres were established at three beaches: Malo-les-Bains, an eastern suburb of Dunkirk (for III Corps); Bray-Dunes Plage, 10km (6 miles) to the east (I Corps); and La Panne Bains (now De Panne), 6km (4 miles) further east (II Corps).

Opposing forces around the Dunkirk–Lille Pocket, 1800hrs 26 May

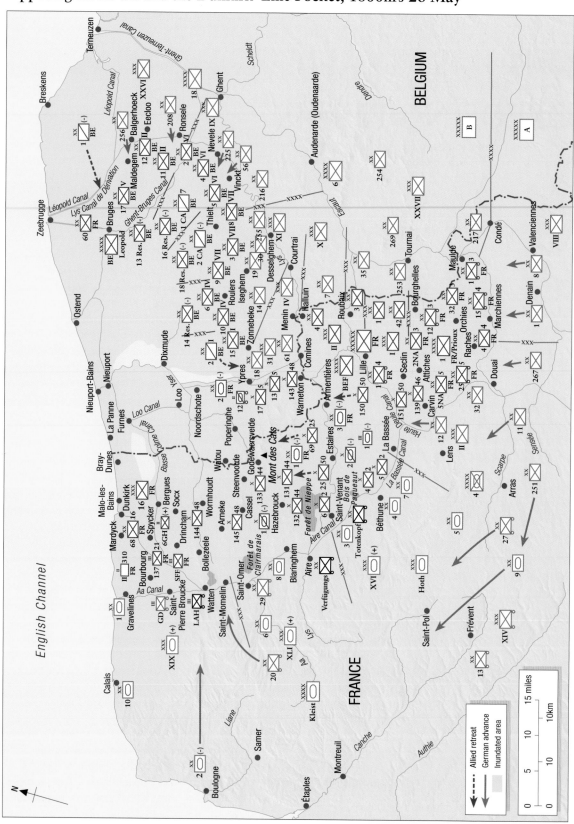

Gort's next task was to organize the orderly withdrawal into the perimeter by forces spread about both sides of the Dunkirk–Lille Pocket. On the eastern front, on the morning of 26 May Gort directed Major-General Harold E. Franklyn to move his 5th Division northwards to man positions along the Comines–Ypres Canal, filling the gap between the Belgians and II Corps. Required to shield the retirement routes of I Corps and rear echelon formations withdrawing from the bottom of the pocket northwards to Dunkirk, this movement was largely carried out by the GHQ motor transport companies. Franklyn's troops would be followed by Major-General Giffard Martel's 50th Division once the GHQ transport returned to pick them up.

On the western side, command of III Corps was passed to Major-General S. R. Wason RA, Gort's chief of artillery. Wason could exercise only limited control over his four divisions since their brigades were scattered in small detachments and communication was problematic. Consequently, he spent most of the next two days attempting to coordinate the withdrawal effort with the French 1ère Armée.

Realizing that there was no option open to him but to follow the British lead, at 2230hrs on 25 May Gén. Blanchard issued the order: 'The 1ère Armée, the BEF and the Belgian Army will regroup progressively behind the water-line demarcated by the Aa Canal, the Lys and the "Canal de Dérivation" so as to form a bridgehead covering Dunkirk in breadth.'

The French plan for the withdrawal was to pull the divisions of 1ère Armée back successively to the Scarpe, Deule Canal and Lys concurrent with the BEF retirements. Separate retreat routes were established for French and British units but because of their relative locations in the pocket and the situation each faced, often these were not used.

In any event Blanchard considered the movement as simply a retreat into a more defensible pocket, a supersized fortress. As his Operational Order No. 30 (26 May) emphasized, 'This bridgehead will be held with no thought of retreat.'

But the British thought only in terms of evacuating their defeated army. Assigned the task of planning for just this contingency, V. Adm. Ramsay had already organized the evacuation of 4,368 troops from Boulogne, 440 from Calais and had returned 23,128 non-combat personnel to England.

Thames motorboats under tow by a Royal Navy tugboat. Because a large number of troops would have to be lifted from the beaches, Ramsay's naval and large personnel vessels were augmented by what became known as the 'little ships'. Note that the davits of the SS *President* are empty. (IWM HU3384)

Dunkirk Harbour when the Royal Navy arrived. The Saint-Pol oil refinery burns fiercely in the background as a paddle-wheel minesweeper steams into the harbour and HMS *Vanquisher* (foreground) positions to do so. The east mole is to the left, with one vessel docked there, and the west mole with its lighthouse is to the right. (IWM C1720)

Protected by his reinforced destroyer flotilla a large contingent of impressed merchant vessels – mainly cross-Channel passenger ferries and railway packet steamers – anchored at Dover, Southampton and the Downs (between Goodwin Sands and the Kent coastline) were organized by Ramsay's hand-picked 16-man *Dynamo* staff. These vessels, called 'personnel ships', were augmented with six 'coasters', 16 motorized barges, five Belgian tugboats and 40 Dutch *schuyts* (squat, flat-bottomed, shallow-draught motorized coastal cargo vessels, called 'skoots' by the British and manned with RN crews) anchored in the Downs, plus 32 naval auxiliaries (motor transport, stores and petrol ships, etc.) At this point Dunkirk's port facilities were still operational and Dover Command planned for these larger vessels to shuttle in convoys departing every four hours between the two ports, and sent the five Belgian tugs ahead to help them manoeuvre in the tight confines of the ancient harbour.

However, because the BEF planned for some embarkation to be done from the beaches east of Dunkirk, the Admiralty realized that a huge number of smaller vessels would be required very soon. To supplement the Dover Command's 76 small craft, four Belgian passenger launches and Ramsgate customs motorboats immediately available, the Small Vessels Pool (SVP) – commanded by Vice Admiral Sir Lionel Preston – gathered 43 pleasure craft near Westminster Pier, but it was obvious these would not be enough. Most of the dozen staff officers of Preston's SVP were dispatched to the principal yachting centres, the Royal Navy Reserve's south-coast training establishment, and the Ports of London and Plymouth to requisition as many seaworthy 'little ships' as could be found. In the next few days, from every port between Plymouth and Hull streams of smaller vessels began to flow, eventually gathering at Ramsgate, anxious to participate in one of the most monumental events in maritime and military history.

It would be the mission of the Air Vice-Marshal Keith Park's 11 Group to provide fighter protection over the port, beaches and ships. To do so, he planned to provide alternating waves of Spitfires and Hurricanes beginning at dawn each day. These would launch at 50-minute intervals (from 0430hrs until 1930hrs) to cover the French coast in squadron strength, typically 12 aircraft. Patrolling beyond the effective range of the new Chain Home radar system, the relatively untested Spitfire and Hurricane pilots would be operating in an aerial no man's land against the battle-hardened *Jagdflieger* of the Luftwaffe.

Evacuation routes X, Y and Z across the English Channel, 26 May to 4 June

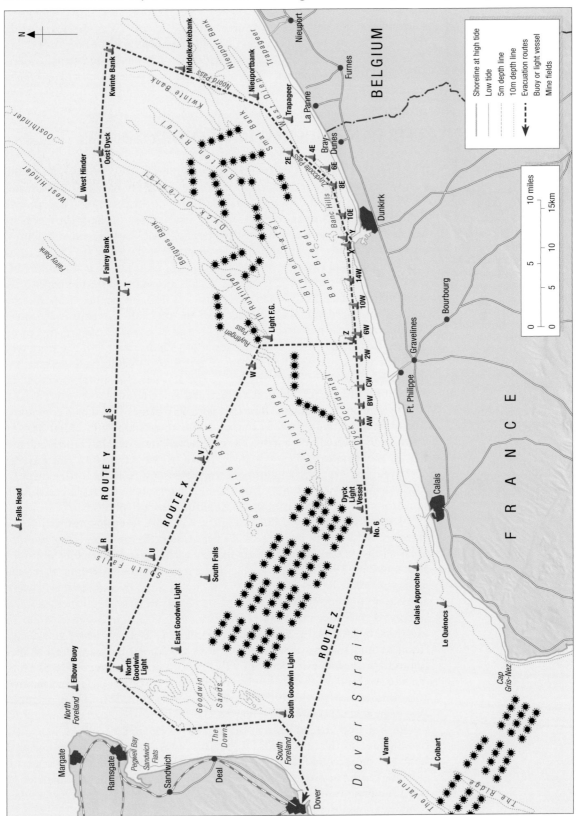

Captain William G. Tennant RN. Chief Staff Officer to the First Sea Lord, Tennant was a former cruiser captain and cruiser squadron commander who had volunteered to assist in the evacuation. He later commanded the battlecruiser HMS *Repulse* and during *Overlord* was in charge of Mulberry (artificial harbour) and PLUTO (undersea pipeline) operations. (© National Portrait Gallery, London)

Nevertheless, a little over two and a half hours after the Panzers were once again unleashed, the Admiralty signalled 'Operation *Dynamo* is to commence'. Throughout the day Ramsay's ongoing shuttle service continued; during the morning two hospital carriers brought home 646 wounded. In the late afternoon six personnel ships arrived, delivering 250 service and signals troops and 12,000 gallons of water, and rescued 3,748 men with the 1,182-ton French steamer *Rouen* taking 420 wounded *poilus* to Cherbourg.

THE PANZERS ROLL, MONDAY 27 MAY

The first full day of Operation *Dynamo*, the Luftwaffe completed the destruction of Dunkirk as an operating seaport. Flying 225 bomber and 75 Stuka sorties and dropping over 350 tons of bombs, four *Fliegerkorps* (I, II, IV and VIII) undertook a series of raids. They began with waves of Heinkel 111s (from KG 1 and 4) pulverizing Dunkirk's harbour facilities, completing the devastation of the seven docking basins, 8km (5 miles) of quays and 47ha (115 acres) of docks and warehouses. The next wave (KG 54) sank the 8,033-ton French steamer *Aden* near the eastern breakwater. At 0740hrs Stukas (StG 2) sank the French 3,047-ton steamer *Côte d'Azur* and an auxiliary minesweeper as well as the 868-ton British 'coaster' *Worthtown*. Finally Dornier 17Zs (KG 2 and 3) wrecked the railway yards and set fire to the town and the Saint-Pol refinery. By noon the port was completely blocked and the fires raged unchecked – killing 1,000 civilians – the huge pall of oily black smoke, rising 3,500m (11,500ft) into the air, providing a beacon for both the raiders and defenders.

Royal Air Force fighters countered with 287 sorties flown in 23 missions, patrolling from Gravelines to Furnes with occasional forays as far east as Ostend and south to Saint-Omer. They accounted for seven Do 17Zs (KG 2 and KG 3), two Ju 88s (II./LG 1) and six He 111s (KG 51, KG 53 and KG 54) destroyed, but lost heavily to the bombers' defensive fire and escorting fighters. Battling 550 Messerschmitts operating in *Gruppe* strength (40 fighters) RAF squadrons lost 14 Hurricanes and five Spitfires in dogfights above the beaches.

More threatening to Allied shipping were the recently captured shore batteries and German heavy artillery near Calais. Passing only 2km (1 mile) offshore east of Calais the 870-ton motor vessel *Sequacity* was hit four times and sank, its 13-man crew being rescued by a tramp steamer that was damaged by the barrages. Two other steamers and a British destroyer were also hit, and three additional ships turned back because of the shellfire.

The route between Dover and Dunkirk being used (later labelled Route Z) was the shortest possible, only 63km (40 miles), considering that Ramsay and Abrial's commands had done their previous mission well: sowing the Channel between the Downs and Nieuport with 5,000 mines in 33 large fields. Skirting them to the south, the route hugged the French coast from Calais to Dunkirk but now German heavy artillery made it unusable in daylight. Dunkirk could also be reached by circumnavigating the fields to the north, steaming to Kwinte Buoy off Ostend before doubling back via Zuydcoote Pass, along the eastern edge of the minefields. While this 140km (87-mile) route exposed Ramsay's ships to the Luftwaffe and S-boats, it avoided the deadly accurate German shore batteries. Accepting the risk, at 1100hrs Ramsay dispatched two personnel ships, two hospital carriers and a pair of destroyers via what would become Route Y.

A shorter route (88.5km, 55 miles, titled Route X) was plotted diagonally from North Goodwin light to the north end of Ruytingen Bank then angling south through the heavily mined Ruytingen Pass. To clear the channel Ramsay sent two minesweepers, a minelaying destroyer (equipped with minesweeping gear) and a lighthouse tender (to mark the route with buoys). These were followed later by two more minesweepers, the anti-aircraft cruiser HMS *Calcutta*, three destroyers and two personnel ships. While these two groups made it safely it was apparent that until Ruytingen Pass could be systematically swept and marked with 'dans' (small flag-topped buoys), the longer, more exposed Route Y would be the primary course between Dunkirk and Dover.

At 1900hrs arriving aboard another destroyer was Captain William G. Tennant, the Senior Naval Officer (SNO–Dunkirk), with 172 RN personnel and a communications staff, to establish the shore parties to control the embarkation process. He quickly assessed the port as unusable – the city was ablaze and the facilities completely destroyed – and signalled Dover, 'Please send every available craft to beaches East of Dunkirk immediately. Evacuation tomorrow night is problematic.'

The latter part of the message was motivated by Brigadier Geoffrey Mansergh, II Corps' chief administrative officer. Aware that the Panzer offensive had resumed, he told Tennant 'we expect the German tanks on the beaches within 24 hours – 36 at the most'. In an effort to rescue as many as possible of the 20,000 rear-area troops then inside the Dunkirk perimeter, Tennant ordered two personnel ships and the destroyers to begin evacuating troops from the beaches using their lifeboats. Responding to the urgent request, at Dover V. Adm. Ramsay ordered four paddle minesweepers and all his available smaller ships – 15 *schuyts* and 17 drifters – to proceed to the beaches and recalled four destroyers patrolling the eastern approaches to the Channel to do the same.

The Panzer offensive on the west side of the pocket had indeed resumed. Early in the morning Guderian hurled 10. Panzer-Division's PR 4 across the Aa at Watten to assault the French infantry battalions at Bollezeele. Even with three battalions of artillery the French regulars were no match for

Léopold III, King of the Belgians. (IWM HU48971)

The Panzers roll again – finally. Panzerkampfwagen IIs from Rommel's PR 25 ('R' on the turret represents the regimental staff of Oberst Rothenburg) cross a pontoon bridge over La Bassée Canal. (IWM RML150)

the armour and by the end of the day were overrun, one battalion (I/48e RI) and some artillery (II/35e RAD and I/115e RALH) surviving and withdrawing to Drincham. Similarly, north of Bourbourg the 1. Panzer-Division pulverized II/137e RI, breaking through in the afternoon to close a steel ring around Gravelines (II/310e RI) and Fort Philippe (VII/310e RI).

Further south Major-General Noel Irwin's 2nd Division attempted to hold a 32km (20-mile) length of canal from Aire to La Bassée. Along this front the full fury of three Panzer and two SS divisions was unleashed. Following a devastating artillery bombardment, in the pre-dawn darkness tanks rolled through the bridgeheads and violently assaulted the scattered British battalions. Without anti-tank guns (all sent to the Dunkirk perimeter) and with very limited artillery (reassigned to II Corps) the defenders were overrun at almost every point.

In the centre of the line, the battalions of the 4th Brigade were battered, surrounded and systematically destroyed by the 4. Panzer-Division and SS-Division 'Totenkopf'. On the right flank the 6th Brigade was overrun by the 3. Panzer-Division and virtually wiped out by noon, the survivors seeking shelter in the Forest of Nieppe. On the left the 5th Brigade was beaten back by Rommel's 7. Panzer-Division. A small futile counterattack briefly spoiled his success, but shortly after noon Rommel launched a powerful coordinated assault that drove an armoured wedge deep towards Armentières, the first step in the encirclement and eventual destruction of the French 1ère Armée at Lille.

Meanwhile on the more desperately threatened east side of the pocket, at the Comines–Ypres Canal, Franklyn's three brigades were hit by the full strength of three infantry divisions. Enemy assaults were powerful and the fighting vicious. In a dramatic see-saw battle the British gave ground and counterattacked repeatedly. Finally, the fighting died down at last about midnight, giving the exhausted British troops some respite before the new day brought renewed German attacks.

With the 5th Division holding throughout the day, I Corps began pulling out of line about 2200hrs with the 1st Division beginning its two-day 95km (60-mile) trek north, all the way to the Dunkirk perimeter, leaving behind three battalions as an emergency reserve for II Corps. The 42nd Division

followed, one brigade, the 125th, stopping to set up a rearguard on the Deule Canal between Lille and Wambrechies while the others, the 126th and 127th, formed the new line on the Lys east of Armentières.

Behind them Major-General Bernard L. Montgomery's 3rd Division began its 40km (25-mile) move to take position on Franklyn's left. Transported by 2,000 troop carriers, lorries, vans and staff cars Montgomery's 13,600 men passed behind the 4th and 5th Divisions and arrived at their new positions at 1000hrs, extending the British line north to near Noordschote. Once Montgomery had passed behind them, the 4th Division retired directly to the west, redeploying behind the Lys west of Warneton. One of its brigades, the 12th, covered the right flank of the neighbouring 5th Division and while the two others, the 10th and 11th, became Franklyn's reserves.

Attempting to close the gap created by the departure of the British divisions, the French 1ère Armèe also began its retirement to the north, but things did not work out so well. Marching on foot, hungry, exhausted, low on ammunition and harried by incessant Luftwaffe attacks, their three corps had to cross the Deule Canal between Provin and Lille in order to reach the new defensive line on the Lys. Unfortunately Général de corps d'armée Aymer's 4e Corps d'armée was only able to withdraw to around Seclin, south of the canal, regrouping the next day. Général de corps d'armée René Altmayer's 5e Corps d'armée came under heavy artillery fire and almost continual air attacks and soon became lost, frustrated and confused. More fortunate was Général de corps d'armée de la Laurencie's 3e Corps d'armée, which had the advantage of following the British divisions north of Lille.

By this time the Belgian Army was being forced into a pocket of its own. Their right flank was pushed back to the north-east near Passchendaele, some 13km (8 miles) from the end of the BEF line at Ypres. Closing in from the east the German XXVI AK penetrated Belgian lines at Maldegem and Ursel. In their centre, two German divisions opened a 7km (4-mile) gap between Thielt and Iseghem, counterattacks were repulsed and the Germans' route to Bruges and Ostend lay open. Communications and transport were in chaos and the throng of refugees – an estimated 3 million people in an area of 1,700km^2 (650 square miles) – made any meaningful manoeuvres impossible.

The Luftwaffe's Messerschmitt Bf 109E dominated the air battles fought over Dunkirk. Fighter sweeps (*frei Jagd*) and bomber escorts (*Jagdschutz*) effectively warded off the RAF fighters, eventually shooting down 30 Hurricanes, 20 Spitfires and six Defiants for the loss of 26 'Emils'. (Courtesy of the Lawrence J. Hickey Collection)

At 1230hrs Léopold telegraphed Lord Gort, 'The time is rapidly approaching when [we] will be unable to continue the fight. [I] will be forced to capitulate to avoid a collapse.' Two hours later the French liaison officers were also informed. With their backs to the sea, ammunition exhausted and the hospitals overflowing the Belgians had done all they could. At 1545hrs Léopold opened negotiations for the surrender of his army and his nation. Shortly after midnight the king accepted Hitler's demand for unconditional capitulation and a ceasefire went into effect at 0400hrs the next morning. The formal surrender document was signed later that day.

THE BELGIANS SURRENDER, TUESDAY 28 MAY

Léopold's capitulation of the Belgian Army created a vacuum of sorts on the eastern side of the Dunkirk–Lille Pocket, though one still crowded with refugees and disarmed troops. The Germans were slow to fill it. Using improvised motor transport the 256. Infanterie-Division did not begin its advance until 1100hrs, allowing the Allies time to cobble together a new defensive line to block them. Key to this new line was Général de brigade Deslaurens' 60e Division d'infanterie, which had been holding the Léopold Canal north of Bruges until alerted the night before that the Belgian collapse was imminent. Leaving their artillery (which had been attached to the Belgian V Corps) Deslaurens' infantry began heading west. Riding in commandeered Belgian lorries the 241e RI made it to Nieuport and established a new line to the south, behind the Yser, but the 270e RI, marching on foot, was caught, surrounded and surrendered the next day.

Hot on the heels of the French, Aufkl.-Abt. 256, a motorcycle-mounted reconnaissance unit, arrived at Nieuport and captured one bridge intact but were halted there by a vicious firefight with the 12th Lancers' armoured cars. Since there was little the Lancers could do against a more formidable assault, a makeshift force of former artillerymen, a battery of four World War I 18-pdrs, some Grenadiers, engineers and support troops (some 550 men altogether) was thrown into the fight at Nieuport.

Inside the perimeter another catastrophe threatened the beachhead. The 2nd Anti-Aircraft Brigade had been withdrawn to Dunkirk days before in order to fend off Luftwaffe attacks on the port and the beaches. With an urgent need for troops to man the perimeter, instructions to the commander, Major-General Henry G. Martin, directed him to send any spare gunners to join the infantry and evacuate the wounded and injured. The message was misunderstood and Martin had all (over 100) 3.7in. anti-aircraft guns disabled and his gunners queued up for evacuation, leaving the air defence of the port and perimeter to smaller 40mm Bofors of the 51st Light Anti-Aircraft Regiment (with a maximum effective vertical range of 1,220m, 4,000ft) and the Tommies' Bren guns.

Built in 1936 for the New Medway Steam Packet Co. the MV *Queen of the Channel* was the first diesel-powered, cross-Channel steamer and was the most modern of the 32 personnel ships impressed into Royal Navy service for Operation *Dynamo*. (1936 postcard from the Ian Boyle Collection www.simplonpc.co.uk)

Fortunately the spiked anti-aircraft guns would not be needed – at least not this day. The weather deteriorated throughout the day with piles of cloud mingling with the pall of oily smoke soon to obscure the harbour and beaches. Only 75 bombing sorties were flown against Dunkirk, the largest raid arriving at 1000hrs – KG 77 Dorniers heavily protected by Bf 109Es. The RAF's 11 Group had learned a lesson the previous day and paired its squadrons to create larger formations, though only by flying half the number of patrols (321 sorties in 11 missions). The Messerschmitt escorts (JG 3, JG 26, JG 51 and JG 54) were numerous and effective, only one Do 17Z was lost to RAF fighters but in this and other sporadic clashes during the day three Spitfires, three Defiants and eight Hurricanes were shot down for the loss of only two Bf 109Es.

While heavy cloud and continuous rain cloaked the Dunkirk perimeter for the rest of the day, clear skies over Lille funnelled heavy Luftwaffe attacks against the French 4e and 5e Corps d'armée. Paralyzed by repeated air raids, Géns. Aymer and Altmayer gave up retreating and elected to fight it out where they stood. Général de la Laurencie, knowing the only hope lay at Dunkirk, continued to lead his 3e Corps d'armée northwards, losing his rearguard (1ère Division d'infanterie motorisée) and one other division (2e Division d'infanterie Nord-Africaine) to the closing pincers formed by 7. Panzer-Division from the west and 7. Infanterie-Division from the east.

At Dunkirk, beneath the blanket of smoke and clouds, the pace of the evacuation began to increase dramatically. Captain Tennant was dissatisfied with the slow, tedious process of plucking small batches of troops from the beaches. The shallow shelving and numerous sandbars prevented larger ships from approaching closer than 800m (2,625ft) and the slow back-breaking rowing of ship's lifeboats required 6–12 hours to fill the ships to capacity. Consequently during the first full day of *Dynamo* only 7,669 troops[1] were evacuated.

At 2200hrs the night before, Capt. Tennant directed one of the personnel ships, the modern 1,162-ton *Queen of the Channel*, to try docking against the harbour side of the Jetée de l'est (known as the 'east mole' to the British). This was a rocky 1,280-metre long (4,200ft) breakwater extending from the base of old fortifications to the harbour's mouth. Atop tall pilings set in the tumbled stone boulders was a wooden gangway about two metres wide. While not designed as a docking or embarkation pier, in the darkness Captain

1. There are five sources for the numbers of personnel evacuated during Operation *Dynamo*, none of which agrees. Used here are the numbers from The Admiralty's Historical Section, which are perhaps not the most accurate but are the highest and therefore the most often quoted. They represent the approximate numbers arriving in England from midnight one day to midnight the next.

German and Allied forces engaged around Dunkirk and Lille, 2200hrs 28 May

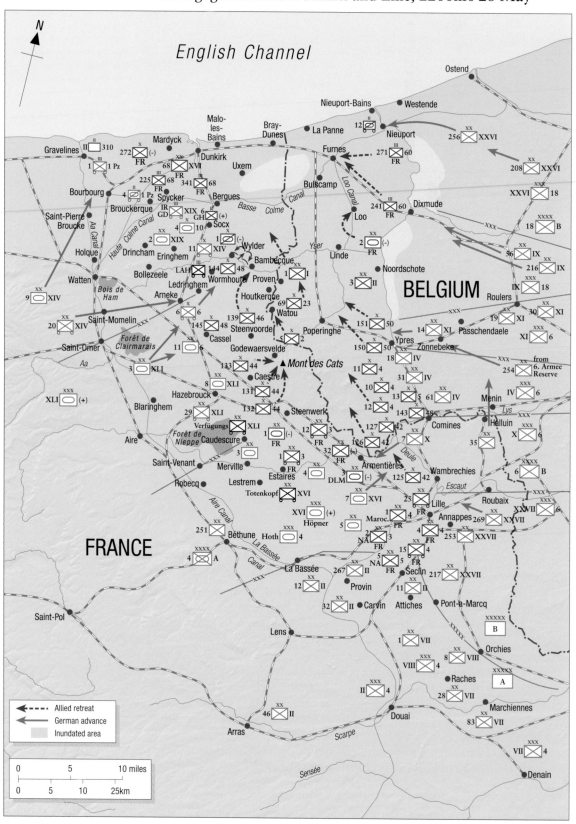

W. J. Odell eased the cross-Channel steamer to the jetty, the crew made fast a head rope and he warped alongside, secured with lines fore and aft. As Tennant watched, 600 troops shuffled down the makeshift dock and boarded *Queen of the Channel* via ladders and gangplanks.

With this success, Tennant and his staff quickly organized berthing parties to secure the ships, set up a control system to manage the flow of men and signalled destroyers to enter the harbour, dock and load. In pairs, six of the nimble warships came alongside, embarked troops and then backed out, turned and headed for Dover at 22 knots. Followed by two others lifting men from the beaches, these were replaced by the four destroyers called in from their patrol stations, four more arriving from the Western Approaches and two others from Portsmouth, beginning a steady continuous cycle of embarkations and departures.

The day's only major loss was the plucky *Queen of the Channel*. Just after dawn and just past halfway to Kwinte Buoy, she was spotted by a lone Ju 88A (from I./KG 30) on an armed reconnaissance sortie and was sent to the bottom, her crew and 904 troops being rescued by the 1,039-ton stores ship *Dorrien Rose*.

With embarkations from the east mole shifting into high gear, at 1100hrs Gén. Blanchard arrived at Gort's CP at Houtkerque to discuss the adjustments needed to compensate for the Belgian capitulation. He was shocked and dismayed to learn that the BEF had orders to evacuate from Dunkirk. Also learning that most French troops were too tired to continue retreating, he directed Général de corps d'armée Prioux to continue fighting where they were and, if nothing else, save the honour of the French Army.

Meanwhile at the Comines–Ypres Canal Franklyn's three tired brigades were again hit by the full strength of three German infantry divisions and another day-long, see-saw battle ensued. Eventually the 17th Brigade was overwhelmed and two of the unit's three battalions were virtually annihilated. A late counterattack by the 4th Division's 10th Brigade prevented the same thing from happening to the 13th Brigade, and a late afternoon rainstorm brought the fighting to a close. Once the fighting had died down at 2100hrs the 4th Division – whose artillery had exhausted all their ammunition in the battle – packed up and continued northwards, marching all night to take its positions on the Dunkirk perimeter.

A heavily loaded drifter makes its best speed for England as Dunkirk continues to burn in the background. These 'little ships' brought home only 28,708 men, but they provided the crucial link in ferrying wet and weary troops from the beaches out to the larger vessels waiting offshore. (IWM HU2108)

North of Ypres, the 3rd Division held the line along the Yser River to Noordschote. They were shelled but not seriously challenged by German infantry who were still making their way through the throng of disarmed Belgian troops and masses of frightened refugees. At 2200hrs Montgomery was ordered to pull back and form a new defensive line between Noordschote and Poperinghe with Martel's 50th Division on his right.

On the western side of the retreat corridor, the 2,500-man remnant of the 2nd Division straggled northwards behind the widely spaced brigades of Major-General Edmund Osborne's 44th Division. It had rained heavily during the night, making the retreat miserable for the Allied troops, but also making the ground very soggy, forcing the 8. Panzer-Division's heavy mechanized vehicles to stay on the roads, limiting their mobility. Nevertheless, German attacks began at dawn, mostly against the 132nd Brigade ensconced in the Forest of Nieppe. They were hammered by heavy shellfire and as SS stormtroopers attacked the outlying units, Panzers drove across the Hazebrouck Canal, forcing the defenders into a series of fighting withdrawals.

The spaces between Osborne's other units allowed German mechanized units to penetrate the line in several places, attacking the battalions from multiple sides simultaneously, eventually forcing them to seek the high ground called Mont des Cats near Godewaersvelde. This dominating position, 10km (6 miles) behind Caestre, was already occupied by two RA field regiments – one each from the 42nd and 44th Divisions – who had provided Osborne's scattered battalions with excellent fire support. The 44th Division rallied to this high ground to dig in and defend it the following day while behind them the 2nd Division's survivors rested at Watou.

Meanwhile, north of Osborne's units Major-General Thorne's 48th Division had a tough time. Defending Wormhoudt, the 144th Brigade was subjected to heavy bombardment before the German attacks – by the 6. Panzer-Division's SR 4 and IR (mot.) 'Leibstandarte SS Adolf Hitler' – commenced at 1000hrs. Relentless assaults overwhelmed one battalion and forced the others to fight their way out with rifle, grenade and bayonet. The battered Tommies regrouped at Bambecque that evening.

At the walled hilltop town of Cassel, 145th Brigade was attacked heavily by PR 11's Skoda 35(t) 10.5-ton light tanks throughout the day. The Czech-made tanks went in without infantry support and suffered grievous losses from the brigade's 24 anti-tank guns and four 18-pdrs (K Battery, 5th Regiment RHA) firing through loopholes in the town's thick medieval walls. Though victorious, by the end of the day the Tommies were surrounded.

At the northern end of the line, the rifle brigade (1. Schützenbrigade) and engineers (Pion. Bat. (mot.) 37) of Guderian's 1. Panzer-Division besieged the French fortress troops (II and VII/310e RI) at Gravelines and Fort Philippe. However, anticipating the 300km (186-mile) movement south-east to join Generaloberst von List's AOK 12 for *Fall Rot*, Guderian withdrew the division's two Panzer regiments to laager along the Samer-Montreuil road near Boulogne.

On the front line Guderian's Panzers were replaced by General der Infanterie Gustav von Wietersheim's XIV AK (mot.). Wietersheim left his three original motorized infantry divisions along the Somme and was given three fresh formations to use against the Dunkirk perimeter – the small 9. Panzer-Division (from Heeresgruppe B's XXXIX AK), the 20. Infanterie-Division (mot.) (from Heeresgruppe B's XVI AK), and the light 11. Schützenbrigade (mot.) fresh from its one-day conquest of Jutland the month before (see Campaign 183: *Denmark and Norway 1940* by the same author, Osprey Publishing Ltd: Oxford, 2007). Wietersheim was also given IR (mot.) 'Grossdeutschland' and IR (mot.) 'Leibstandarte SS Adolf Hitler', two battalions of Guderian's heavy artillery and his observation aircraft squadrons.

While the German commanders nearest Dunkirk reorganized their forces, the evacuations continued unabated. The loss of *Queen of the Channel* prompted V. Adm. Ramsay to discontinue the use of large steamers during 'hours of full daylight' and dispatched a dozen more minesweepers and 18 *schuyts*, some of them delivering ammunition, food, medical supplies and 10,000 gallons of water before picking up waiting troops. These, plus a total of 16 destroyers, returned with more of the 11,874 British troops embarked from the harbour and 5,930 from the beaches. Of the total at least 461 were wounded. Additionally, a small convoy of French supply ships evacuated 2,500 'specialist' troops and 480 wounded. Although one ship, the 2,954-ton *Douaisien*, was lost to a magnetic mine, almost all of the 1,000 aboard were rescued.

During the day, however, arrivals outpaced embarkations as another 50,000 men trudged into the perimeter. Most of these were rear echelon and combat support troops. They lacked the unit cohesion and individual discipline of fighting units and soon overwhelmed Tennant's slim staff, one of whom referred to them as 'the odds and ends of an army, not the fighting soldiers'. Added to these were a throng of individual soldiers and small units separated from their larger formations and, in the absence of orders or leadership, simply headed for the funeral pyre of Dunkirk.

To rescue as many as possible as soon as possible, that night Ramsay ordered a maximum effort. To the harbour he sent seven personnel ships, three hospital carriers and two additional destroyers. To the beaches he sent 20 destroyers, 19 minesweepers, 20 *schuyts*, 17 drifters, five coasters and two tugs towing 18 motorboats and 26 lifeboats.

While weather and darkness precluded further Luftwaffe intervention, it encouraged the Kriegsmarine to attempt interdicting this large flow of shipping between Dunkirk and Dover. The north-east corner of Route Y was only 60km (37 miles) from the S-boats' forward base at Flushing and late that afternoon, under a mantle of dark grey skies, three of the fast attack craft departed, cruising stealthily through the scattered rain squalls to take station off Kwinte Buoy hoping to locate and sink some of the many ships passing the well-lit turning point. Their success would be the first of two major disasters to befall the Royal Navy the following day.

7

6

KWINTE BUOY

12 10 3
       9   6
          8
5   6   8
        4   7

D

C

B

A

2

DIRECT ROUTE FROM
FLUSHING TO KWINTE BUOY

1

⊕ z

ROYAL NAVY AND SUPPORTING UNITS
1 Destroyer HMS *Wakeful* (Commander Ralph L. Fisher)
2 Minesweeper HMS *Gossamer* (Lieutenant-Commander Richard C. V. Ross)
3 Minesweeper HMS *Lydd* (Lieutenant-Commander Rodolf C. D. Haig)
4 Destroyer HMS *Grafton* (Commander Cecil E. C. Robinson)
5 LNER Channel Ferry *Malines* (Captain G. G. Mallory)
6 Danlayer *Comfort* (Skipper J. D. Mair, RNR)
7 Drifter *Nautilus*
8 Destroyer HMS *Javelin* (Commander Anthony F. Pugsley)
9 Destroyer HMS *Icarus* (Commander Colin D. Maud)
10 Destroyer HMS *Vanquisher* (Lieutenant-Commander C. Byron Alers-Hankey)
11 Destroyer HMS *Intrepid* (Commander Roderick C. Gordon)
12 Destroyer HMS *Ivanhoe* (Commander Philip H. Hadow)

GERMAN FORCES
S-boats
A S.30 (Oberleutnant zur See Wilhelm Zimmerman)
B S.25 (Kapitänleutnant Siegried Wuppermann)
C S.34 (Oberleutnant zur See Albrecht Obermaier)

U-boat
D U.62 (Oberleutnant zur See Hans-Bernard Michalowski)

13 1321hrs: *U.60* attacks Polish destroyer *Blyskawica* at N 51° 19'/E 02° 07' while the latter was operating with three British destroyers. All torpedoes miss. *U.60* is depth-charged but sustains no damage.

Notes:
 1. The wreckage of *Grafton* now lies in 24m of water at 51° 24' 28" N/02° 49' 10" E.
 2. The wreckage of *Wakeful* now lies in 17.5m of water at 51° 22' 44" N/02° 43' 22" E.

Richthofen's dreaded Stukas peeling off into a dive. While deadly, these assets were available in limited numbers, their operations having to be divided between the evacuation fleet off Dunkirk and the Allied ground forces – such as Maj. Gen. Osborne's 44th Division and the French 1ère Armée – located well inland. (IWM, HU58529)

Conversely the Luftwaffe's dive-bombers were able to operate with near impunity. Tasked to attack 'the numerous merchant vessels in the adjacent sea area [to Dunkirk] and the warships escorting them', at 1500hrs 180 Ju 87s from VIII Fliegerkorps (now reinforced with StG 1) arrived overhead. These were intercepted by a single squadron (No. 56) of Hurricanes who lost two to the rear gunners without shooting down any of the attackers. Thirty minutes later these were followed by dive-bombing Ju 88s from I./KG 30 and II./LG 1. Another 55 Ju 87s (I./StG 2 and II./StG 77) returned at 1830–1855hrs to complete the maelstrom of destruction. (Three were lost to various causes during this attack.)

Targeting the many stationary vessels embarking troops from the jetty and standing just offshore, this devastating series of attacks sank one destroyer and damaged five others so badly they were withdrawn for repairs (55 RN personnel killed and 114 wounded). Off Bray-Dunes, the 1,105-ton escort sloop HMS *Bideford* had 12m (40ft) of her stern completely blown off (with 16 crew and 12 troops killed, 20 crewmen wounded) and was beached to prevent sinking. On the return route two ancient 500-ton paddle-wheel minesweepers were also lost, one going down with 360 troops and most of its crew. Five personnel ships and three small trawlers were also sunk by air attack. The largest lost was the 6,787-ton Glasgow merchantman SS *Clan Macalister*, which arrived off Malo-les-Bains with eight new army assault landing craft. After they brought the first load of troops to the ship it was hit repeatedly and, burning fiercely, had to be abandoned.

The heavy Stuka attack also caught the French's first *Dynamo* evacuation ships – three 1,298-ton destroyers of the 6e Division de torpilleurs – in the harbour, damaging the *Mistral* so badly she was withdrawn from action. The other two embarked 1,084 troops – with the *Cyclone* also rescuing 158 Tommies from a sinking British minesweeper – before escaping. The French also lost two large (3,200-ton) and two small (750-ton) steamers, and three of the Belgian tugboats were sunk.

In spite of these heavy losses, 18 destroyers, ten personnel ships, nine minesweepers and an increasing number of smaller vessels returned with 47,310 men, of which about 1,880 were wounded. Some 13,752 were lifted from the beaches. The largest contingent – 1,856 troops – was brought home by the anti-aircraft cruiser *Calcutta*, which had been stationed off La Panne to protect GHQ, the evacuation beach and shipping gathered there. Having exhausted its ammunition (with negligible results) the ship received troops ferried to it by a tug, two minesweepers and eight smaller ships before heading to Dover for replenishment.

While the Luftwaffe struck at Dunkirk, at Rundstedt's HQ in Charleville, Generaloberst Walter von Brauchitsch (commander-in-chief of the German army), and his chief of staff, Gen.Maj. Halder, met with the Heeresgruppe A commanders to brief the OKH's deployment directive for *Fall Rot*. Having signed the order the day before, Hitler and his OKW staff flew to Cambrai aerodrome where, Kesselring reported, after the Führer's monologue, in which he 'expressed his special thanks to all ranks… [and informed the commanders] of his future intentions', the plan was briefed to the Heeresgruppe B commanders. As soon as the generals could return to their HQs, movement orders flew to their subordinate formations, realigning the armies and air fleets for the assault across the Somme, inevitably taking their attention away from Dunkirk.

Meanwhile the Allies' 48km-long (30-mile) defensive perimeter began to take shape, and just in time. During the previous evening the main body of the 256. Infanterie-Division arrived before Nieuport and began preparations

for a serious assault. Fortunately about this time the 4th Division's 12th Brigade and 22nd Field Regiment RA (with 24 25-pdrs) arrived having marched all night from the Lys. They relieved the beleaguered and exhausted group of gunners, lancers and grenadiers, and repulsed the attackers.

Falling in on the 12th Brigade's right was the 10th Brigade, straight from the hard fighting along the Comines–Ypres Canal the day before. No rest for the weary, Brigadier Anderson's men were soon confronted by the 208. Infanterie-Division. Later still the 11th Brigade moved into position on Anderson's right, extending the line further towards Furnes, just as the bicycle-mounted reconnaissance troops (Radfahrer Schwadron 25) of the 56. Infanterie-Division approached that sector.

Also tramping into the perimeter was Major-General Harry Curtis's small 46th Division. This understrength and undertrained unit lacked artillery and anti-tank guns and could not be expected to withstand a serious assault. Nevertheless it was one of the freshest and most cohesive units available and was deployed along the Basse Colme Canal from Bergues through to Hoymille.

While the 3rd and 50th Divisions held the line from Noordschote to Poperinghe, the more substantial surviving elements of the 5th and 42nd Divisions fell back into the last rearguard line from Linde to Bambecque on the Yser. Through these lines filed the retreating units of the BEF, led by Major-General the Hon. Harold R. L. G. Alexander's 1st Division. Throughout the day the 1st Guards and 3rd Brigades took up positions along the Basse Colme Canal while the 2nd Brigade went into reserve near Bray-Dunes.

Following were the sad survivors of Maj. Gen. Irwin's 2nd Division, who trudged to Malo-les-Bains to begin evacuating since they had negligible combat strength left anyway. Crossing the canal on the Pont-aux-Cerfs bridge to Bray-Dunes, weary and wounded soldiers passed their weapons, mostly Bren guns, to the grim but relatively fresh defenders, the 3rd Brigade's 1st Battalion The Duke of Wellington's Regiment.

South of the BEF's rearguard, the badly mauled 44th Division and 145th Brigade attempted to evacuate their positions and rejoin Gort's forces. After a pulverizing Stuka attack at 0600hrs by 60 Ju 87Bs that caused over 100 casualties, Maj. Gen. Osborne knew that his battered units would not withstand the Panzer assault that was surely coming. Organized into two columns, Osborne's battered division departed Mont des Cats at 1000hrs and reached the beaches the next day.

Surrounded at Cassel, the 145th Brigade's commander, Brigadier the Hon. Nigel F. Somerset, did not receive his orders to withdraw until early that morning. By then it was too late to do so – lest they be caught and annihilated on the move in broad daylight – and the orders were changed to hold the hilltop town until the following night.

HELL FROM ABOVE, 29 MAY 1940 (pp. 54–55)

As the third wave of dive-bombers approached Dunkirk harbour, they were immediately attracted to the ten vessels clustered at the end of the eastern jetty. Berthed on the harbour-side of the mole were (from the end, landward) the destroyer *Grenade* (Commander Richard C. Boyle), six armed trawlers of Minesweeping Groups 51 and 61 (Sub-Lieutenant Robin Bill, aboard *Fyldea*) moored in two rows of three and the destroyer *Verity* (Commander Robert H. Mills). Along the sea side of the jetty were the large Isle of Man packet RMS *Fenella* (Captain W. Cubbon) and paddle-wheel Thames excursion steamer *Crested Eagle* (Lieutenant-Commander Bernard R. Booth, RNR).

Beginning their attacks at 1750hrs, *Grenade* **(1)** was soon hit twice, one bomb exploding in a forward fuel tank and starting raging internal fires. Fourteen ratings were killed and another four mortally wounded. Recognizing the ship was doomed, Cdr. 'Jack' C. Clouston's Royal Naval 'pier party' slipped the ship's lines so that it would not sink at its berth but the tide swung it around until it drifted stern-first into harbour channel.

Meanwhile *Fenella* **(2)**, having embarked 650 troops, had a bomb plunge through her promenade deck, killing 15. Two other bombs hit the mole alongside exploding among the jetty's boulders, wrecking the engine room and perforating her hull below the waterline. The ship began to settle and list and those on board evacuated forward onto the *Crested Eagle*. *Fenella* slowly sank at its berth.

Another salvo of bombs rained down upon the trawlers. The *Polly Johnson* (Lieutenant F. Padley, RNR; outboard in the first row) was heavily damaged by two near misses that wiped out

the 3in. gun crew and she soon departed in company with *Arley* (Skipper A. Duffield, RNR), but had to be abandoned and scuttled en route. The *Brock* (Skipper A. U. Setterfield, RNR) also got under way, leaving *Fyldea* **(3)** (Skipper G. Whammond, RNR) moored to the mole. The *Calvi* **(4)** (Skipper Bertram D. Spindler, RNR; outboard in the second row) had a bomb go down a ventilator shaft and through its bottom and sank upright.

Further down the jetty, *Verity* had been straddled by bombs for about 35 minutes when Cdr. Mills, seeing that the air attacks had driven the troops from the mole, got under way empty, skirting the burning *Grenade* and the *Calvi*'s wreckage as she left the harbour.

Loaded with 600 shell-shocked troops *Crested Eagle* **(5)** got under way at approximately 1830hrs, pulling away from the mole in a wide turn to port and was pounced upon by the last of the Stukas. Four bombs rained upon it setting the aft end of the ancient wooden ship fiercely ablaze. Lieutenant-Commander Booth quickly realized his ship was doomed and ran the burning wreck aground near Zuydcoote Sanitorium where the 200 surviving troops and crew – many of them severely burned – were rescued by three minesweepers and the destroyer *Sabre*.

Meanwhile, fearing that the sinking, blazing *Grenade* would block the harbour channel, Cdr. Clouston ordered trawler *John Cattling* **(6)** (Skipper G. W. Aldan, DSC, RNR) to tow *Grenade* out of the channel. Burning fiercely from stem to stern, *Grenade* was pulled to the west side of the outer harbour where, at approximately 2000hrs, her magazines exploded.

Meanwhile the trap closed around the French 1ère Armée. Driving from the west Höpner's XVI AK (mot.) met Wäger's XXVII AK coming from the east, near Armentières, and closed the trap on six depleted French divisions. The cavalier Gén. Prioux was captured at his command post at Steenwerk and, on 1 June, Général de division Molinié would finally surrender his 35,000 troops when ammunition, food and water were exhausted. In recognition of the defenders' courageous and valiant fight, the Germans allowed them to march out with their colours flying.

At Dover Operation *Dynamo* was almost derailed by two near-simultaneous communiqués. The first was a panicked telephone call from a Royal Navy shore party officer. At 1900hrs Commander J. S. Dove telephoned from La Panne to report that the harbour was once again unusable, blocked by sunken vessels. Lacking radio contact with Tennant and having no way of confirming the distressing news, V. Adm. Ramsay ordered all the ships headed for Dunkirk that night to avoid the harbour and lift troops from the beaches.

An hour later First Sea Lord Admiral of the Fleet Sir Dudley Pound dealt Ramsay another blow. Shocked by the loss of and heavy damage to ten destroyers that day (two sunk by the Kriegsmarine, six knocked out by the Luftwaffe and two severely damaged in accidents) and fearing further losses would soon cripple the Navy for the lack of convoy escorts, Sir Dudley withdrew the seven surviving large destroyers from Dover Command. This left Ramsay with only 13 small World War I destroyers – reinforced by three more arriving from Plymouth – with limited deck space and paltry anti-aircraft defences. Minus the larger destroyers and without the east mole to use, the smaller destroyers, minesweepers, *schuyts* and little ships lifting exhausted men from the waters off the exposed beaches would have to work.

Fortunately they would not have to sail using the long and perilous Route Y. Once the heavy artillery of the 256. Infanterie-Division and XXVI AK (AR 256 and 785) arrived at Nieuport, they quickly saw that the stream of ships passing offshore was well within reach of their 15.5cm and 21cm guns. During the day many vessels were taken under fire and though both British and French destroyers duelled with the batteries, this route now had the same risks that forced the abandonment of Route Z. Finally the sweeping and marking of Route X through the minefields was completed and at 1606hrs Ramsay ordered all *Dynamo* vessels to use Route X, 'exercising navigational caution'.

Former commander of the battleship HMS *Revenge*, on the Admiralty staff Rear Admiral William Frederick Wake-Walker was conspicuously successful in quickly countering the German magnetic mine threat. A tireless leader later noted for hounding the *Bismarck* with his 1st Cruiser Sqn., he was promoted to vice admiral and named Third Sea Lord in April 1942. (IWM A23581)

With the east mole once again open for embarkations, the HMS *Vivacious* comes alongside, squeezing between the jetty and the wreck of the 363-ton armed minesweeping trawler *Calvi* which was sunk during the bombing the day before. Note another destroyer has docked to the seaward side of the breakwater and as yet there are no troops to load. (IWM HU1149)

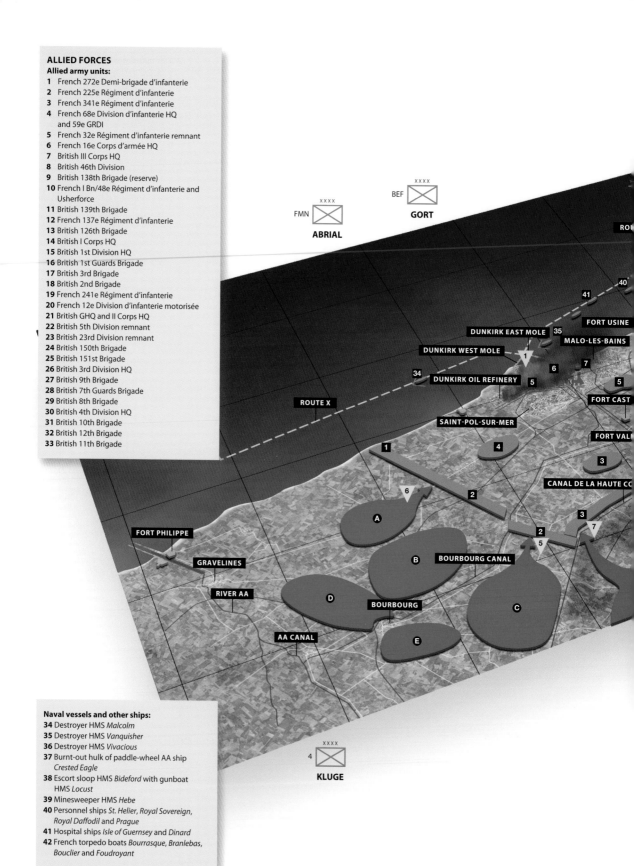

ALLIED FORCES
Allied army units:
1 French 272e Demi-brigade d'infanterie
2 French 225e Régiment d'infanterie
3 French 341e Régiment d'infanterie
4 French 68e Division d'infanterie HQ
   and 59e GRDI
5 French 32e Régiment d'infanterie remnant
6 French 16e Corps d'armée HQ
7 British III Corps HQ
8 British 46th Division
9 British 138th Brigade (reserve)
10 French I Bn/48e Régiment d'infanterie and
   Usherforce
11 British 139th Brigade
12 French 137e Régiment d'infanterie
13 British 126th Brigade
14 British I Corps HQ
15 British 1st Division HQ
16 British 1st Guards Brigade
17 British 3rd Brigade
18 British 2nd Brigade
19 French 241e Régiment d'infanterie
20 French 12e Division d'infanterie motorisée
21 British GHQ and II Corps HQ
22 British 5th Division remnant
23 British 23rd Division remnant
24 British 150th Brigade
25 British 151st Brigade
26 British 3rd Division HQ
27 British 9th Brigade
28 British 7th Guards Brigade
29 British 8th Brigade
30 British 4th Division HQ
31 British 10th Brigade
32 British 12th Brigade
33 British 11th Brigade

Naval vessels and other ships:
34 Destroyer HMS *Malcolm*
35 Destroyer HMS *Vanquisher*
36 Destroyer HMS *Vivacious*
37 Burnt-out hulk of paddle-wheel AA ship
   Crested Eagle
38 Escort sloop HMS *Bideford* with gunboat
   HMS *Locust*
39 Minesweeper HMS *Hebe*
40 Personnel ships *St. Helier, Royal Sovereign,
   Royal Daffodil* and *Prague*
41 Hospital ships *Isle of Guernsey* and *Dinard*
42 French torpedo boats *Bourrasque, Branlebas,
   Bouclier* and *Foudroyant*

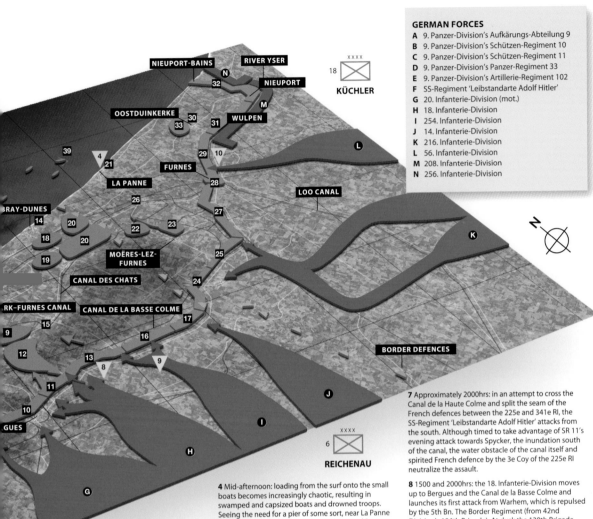

GERMAN FORCES
- **A** 9. Panzer-Division's Aufkärungs-Abteilung 9
- **B** 9. Panzer-Division's Schützen-Regiment 10
- **C** 9. Panzer-Division's Schützen-Regiment 11
- **D** 9. Panzer-Division's Panzer-Regiment 33
- **E** 9. Panzer-Division's Artillerie-Regiment 102
- **F** SS-Regiment 'Leibstandarte Adolf Hitler'
- **G** 20. Infanterie-Division (mot.)
- **H** 18. Infanterie-Division
- **I** 254. Infanterie-Division
- **J** 14. Infanterie-Division
- **K** 216. Infanterie-Division
- **L** 56. Infanterie-Division
- **M** 208. Infanterie-Division
- **N** 256. Infanterie-Division

Map labels: NIEUPORT-BAINS, RIVER YSER, NIEUPORT, 18 KÜCHLER, WULPEN, OOSTDUINKERKE, FURNES, LA PANNE, LOO CANAL, BRAY-DUNES, MOËRES-LEZ-FURNES, CANAL DES CHATS, RK-FURNES CANAL, CANAL DE LA BASSE COLME, BORDER DEFENCES, GUES, REICHENAU

EVENTS

1 Dawn: after devastating Luftwaffe air attacks the previous day, the fourth day of *Dynamo* opens with fog, low overcast skies and a thick pall of oil smoke over Dunkirk harbour. These conditions preclude air raids but the previous day's damage to the east mole initially discourages evacuations from the harbour. HMS *Vanquisher* investigates and finds the mole damaged but still useable. Despite the late start, 24,311 troops are evacuated from the harbour during the day.

2 Midday: gunboat HMS *Locust* begins to tow the severely damaged escort sloop HMS *Bideford* back to England. They arrive 36 hours later.

3 1415hrs: steaming via Route Y four French torpedo boats evacuate troops from Quai Félix Faure. At 1645hrs the *Bourrasque*, while dodging German artillery fire off Nieuport, leaves the swept channel, hits a mine and sinks with the loss of 150 men.

4 Mid-afternoon: loading from the surf onto the small boats becomes increasingly chaotic, resulting in swamped and capsized boats and drowned troops. Seeing the need for a pier of some sort, near La Panne Lieutenant Harold J. Dibbens leads the 102nd Provost Company and Royal Engineers' 250th Field Company in pushing a line of lorries and other abandoned vehicles into the surf, shooting the tires to prevent them from becoming buoyant and lashing planking across their tops to form the first 'provost jetty', jutting some 150m (492ft) into the surf. So successful is this effort that on the evening of 30/31 May, another nine 'provost jetties' are constructed between Malo-les-Bains and La Panne.

5 1400–2000hrs: ordered to drive back the French 225e RI in order to bring their 10.5cm artillery into range of Dunkirk Harbour, light tanks from the 9. Panzer-Division's PR 33 assist their SR 11 in attacking towards Spycker. Artillery bombardment begins at noon, followed by assaults two hours later. However, determined French defence, utilizing its well-emplaced artillery and anti-tank batteries, holds its ground. A follow-up attack at 2000hrs, attempting to use nightfall to their advantage, is similarly repulsed.

6 Later in the evening: to draw off French forces defending against SR 11's attacks, 9. Panzer-Division's Aüfkl-Abt. 9 attacks across the disused Mardyck Canal. Again the French troops, heavily supported by artillery and anti-tank guns, repulse the assaults.

7 Approximately 2000hrs: in an attempt to cross the Canal de la Haute Colme and split the seam of the French defences between the 225e and 341e RI, the SS-Regiment 'Leibstandarte Adolf Hitler' attacks from the south. Although timed to take advantage of SR 11's evening attack towards Spycker, the inundation south of the canal, the water obstacle of the canal itself and spirited French defence by the 3e Coy of the 225e RI neutralize the assault.

8 1500 and 2000hrs: the 18. Infanterie-Division moves up to Bergues and the Canal de la Basse Colme and launches its first attack from Warhem, which is repulsed by the 5th Bn. The Border Regiment (from 42nd Division's 126th Brigade). At dusk the 139th Brigade begins to pull out of the line to move to Malo-les-Bains for evacuation, their place being taken by the French 137e RI. A renewed attack at 2000hrs, in coordination with the attacks by units on the western side of the perimeter, successfully establishes a bridgehead but fierce French counterattacks drive the Germans back across the canal.

9 1600hrs: arriving at the Canal de la Basse Colme, the 254. Infanterie-Division hastily goes into the assault, attempting to cross the canal at two places and relieve pressure on the 18. Infanterie-Division to the west. However, the British defence is stout and the 2nd Coldstream Guards beat back the western attack while the 1st Duke of Wellingtons defeat the one launched from Hondschoote.

10 2200hrs: after an initial repulse late in the day and under a strong artillery bombardment, in the early darkness elements of the 56. Infanterie-Division wade across the canal and infiltrate British defences north of Furnes, establishing a bridgehead. Once discovered, a determined counterattack by the 1st Coldstream Guards drives the Germans back across the canal and restores the defensive line.

THE DUNKIRK PERIMETER IS CLOSED, 30 MAY 1940

The Dunkirk defensive perimeter as it was established on 30 May 1940, the Allied forces within it, harbour embarkation facilities, the three beach evacuation points and the German units facing and attacking the perimeter.

Returning with some 880 troops aboard, the French destroyer *Bourrasque* used Route Y to reduce the collision risk posed by hordes of small ships approaching Dunkirk on Route X. Dodging German shellfire off Nieuport Capitaine R. G. A. Fouqué inadvertently manoeuvred out of the swept channel and hit a mine at 1645hrs, the ship capsizing and sinking 15 minutes later. Only 300 troops and 122 crewmen were rescued. (IWM HU2280)

THE PANZERS TURN AWAY, THURSDAY 30 MAY

Luckily for the Allies, on the German side there was 'the impression here that nothing is happening today, that no one is any longer interested in Dunkirk'. This of course was due to the sudden change of direction occasioned by the *Fall Rot* deployment order. Although Kluge's AOK 4 HQ (whose operations officer, Oberstleutnant Rolf Wuthmann, is quoted above) directed Kleist to close to within artillery range for his 10.5cm guns, this command was busy organizing its new formations. Having lost Guderian's and Reinhardt's Panzer corps, the *Panzergruppe* HQ was now establishing communications with newly-assigned XVI AK (mot.) (Höpner) and XL AK (Stumme) and preparing to move to its new positions east of Amiens. Although Kleist retained Wietersheim's XIV AK (mot.), this command's newly assigned units were not fully in place. When Rundstedt's HQ pressed for an attack at 1500hrs, Kluge's staff replied that XIV AK (mot.) were ready (which they were not) but they needed Heeresgruppe B's AOK 6 to attack in support and these divisions had 'apparently pulled out to rest!'

With a renewed emphasis on attacking the perimeter defences and pushing to the seashore, Kleist got XIV AK (mot.) re-energized but 9. Panzer-Division found the terrain difficult and the French defence (225e RI) stubborn and made little progress. Generalleutnant Mauriz Wiktorim zu Hainburg (20. Infanterie-Division (mot.) commander) was told that he 'must without fail reach the coast today!' but his attacks were repulsed by the French 341e RI. In any event, the effort was stillborn because the XIV AK (mot.)'s medium artillery (the 10.5cm guns) had run out of ammunition the day before!

Contrary to statements by Kluge's staff, Reichenau's AOK 6 was not resting. Three divisions, the 14., 18. and 56. Infanterie-Divisionen, launched assaults across the Basse Colme Canal in the mid-afternoon (at 1500hrs and 1600hrs). The 56. Infanterie-Division was repulsed by Montgomery's 7th Guards Brigade, which had just deployed in and east of Furnes. After sunset (at 2000hrs and 2200hrs) attacks by the 18. and 56. Infanterie-Divisionen resumed but only established tenuous bridgeheads that were thrown back across the canal through spirited counterattacks by the French 137e RI and a battalion of Coldstream Guards.

Because the harbour was deemed unusable, for the only time in the operation more troops were lifted from the beaches than from Dunkirk. The process was aided by the fact that most of the men were from combat units and maintained their discipline in spite of the horrendous conditions. (IWM HU41240)

Overall the day finally proved that the Germans' disjointed and dysfunctional command arrangements were unsatisfactory and OKH ordered a complete restructuring of the forces arrayed against Dunkirk. General der Artillerie Georg von Küchler's AOK 18 was assigned responsibility for all operations against the 'trapped' Allied units and he was given four corps to work with. These contained seven infantry divisions, a motorized rifle brigade and the small, lightweight 9. Panzer-Division. Küchler's reserves consisted of the 20. Infanterie-Division (mot.), IR (mot.) 'Grossdeutschland' and IR (mot.) 'Leibstandarte SS Adolf Hitler'. While this realignment was ordered to be made effective by 0200hrs on the 31st, in those days these sorts of sweeping changes (literally) did not happen overnight and much of the following day was spent rewiring the communications network to put Küchler in touch with his new subordinate units.

To cap off a day of desultory efforts, bad weather grounded the Luftwaffe. Low clouds, fog and mist cloaked the entire coastal area with ceilings of 100m (328ft) and horizontal visibility of 100m. The tops of the cloud blanket were at 1,000m (3,280ft), completely precluding bombing operations. Fighter Command's 11 Group flew 257 sorties in nine missions but these encountered nothing but individual long-range reconnaissance aircraft, two Do 17s being shot down for no losses to enemy action.

Out of view to the left members of the 7th Guards Brigade hunker down in their trench across the t'Coolenhof farm, shielding themselves against an ongoing artillery barrage, their .303-cal. SMLE (Small Magazine Lee Enfield) rifles at the ready on the forward edge of a trench. In the background a portion of Furnes burns from the bombardment. (IWM HU1134)

While confusion, distraction and bad weather hobbled their enemy, during the morning the Allies continued to straggle into the perimeter and embark in the thousands from the beaches between Dunkirk and La Panne. Major-General Martel's 50th Division relieved Franklyn's battered 5th Division between Bulscamp and Pont-aux-Cerfs, allowing the latter to move to an assembly area near the beach. This line had little depth because behind it Les Moëres (a reclaimed sea marsh 4.8km [3 miles] wide and as much as 4.5m [15ft] deep) had been inundated, but it was bolstered by the remaining Somua heavy tanks of the 2e Division légère mécanique, which were positioned along the canal line as steel pillboxes.

Going directly to the beaches for embarkation were Osborne's largely depleted 44th Division and the 23rd Division's sole surviving 69th Brigade. The brigades of the 42nd Division were to have followed, but the need for additional troops to stiffen the weak 46th Division forced Maj. Gen. Wason to divert the 126th Brigade to fill the gap between Alexander's and Curtis's divisions.

Also marching into the Dunkirk perimeter were the exhausted *poilus* of Gén. de la Laurencie's badly depleted 3e Corps. These consisted of two regiments of the 12e Division d'infanterie motorisée with three artillery batteries, two and a half battalions of the 32e Division d'infanterie, two tractor-drawn artillery regiments (15e RADT and 215e RALHT) from the 1ère Division d'infanterie motorisée, two divisional reconnaissance groups, and two squadrons of tanks from the 1ère Division légère mécanique.

By noon the only major British unit south of the perimeter was Brigadier Somerset's 145th Brigade at Cassel. As darkness fell at 2130hrs the dauntless defenders moved out north-eastwards in a single column. However, they soon stumbled into elements of PR 11 – which was laagering in preparation for the southward move – and in a series of running battles through the night, the column fragmented into small groups. After sunrise Somerset, 40 officers and almost 2,000 troops were surrounded and surrendered near Watou. The remainder dispersed, finally straggling into the perimeter two to four days later.

The evacuation – initially limited to lifting troops from the beaches – got off to a slow start this day. Huge numbers of troops on some beaches became frustrated and unruly at the lack of ships and the few ships present waited offshore empty beaches. Just after midnight Rear Admiral W. F. Wake-Walker

The French Navy lost four of their '1500-tonne' torpedo boat destroyers during *Dynamo*, two of them, *Cyclone* and *Siroco* (seen here), being torpedoed by German S-boats on the same morning. These 1,298-ton warships mounted four 5.1in. guns and six torpedo tubes. (1933 Laurent Nel postcard from the author's collection)

arrived with an additional 83 RN personnel and, most importantly, a workable set of radios. The reinforced shore parties were able to restore some order and the radios brought a brief respite to the chronic communications failures.

At first light V. Adm. Ramsay sent the destroyer *Vanquisher* into the harbour to evaluate the east mole. At 0551hrs Lieutenant Commander Conrad B. Alers-Hankey reported that while there were obstructions approaching and damage to the jetty, it was still usable. Taking a cautious 'one ship at a time' approach throughout most of the day, only two personnel ships, three drifters and seven destroyers lifted troops from the harbour. After 1800hrs the tempo returned with ten destroyers (four of them returning for their second load), four personnel ships, a hospital carrier and two *schuyts* embarking troops from the east mole while a collection of 31 miscellaneous vessels and another dozen motorboats went to the beaches.

Finally, at 1530hrs, realizing the desperate nature of the situation and the need to complete the evacuation promptly, Adm. Pound returned five of the larger destroyers (two others in repair) to Ramsay's command. Without hindrance from the Luftwaffe the embarkations once again moved into high gear, helped by the increased efforts of the French Navy. That morning five 630-ton French Élan-class dispatch boats had entered the harbour followed by three torpedo boats and two destroyers, one of the latter being lost to a mine on its return voyage. Later a tug, two minesweepers and seven fishing vessels (Belgian with French Navy crews) arrived. In the afternoon a convoy of five French cargo ships evacuated 3,000 troops.

Beneath the low clouds, patchy fog and light rain some 53,823 troops were rescued, of whom 8,616 were French. For the first time the numbers lifted from the beaches – 29,512 – exceeded those embarked from Dunkirk, due primarily to the night's misguided moratorium denying use of the harbour. Among those aboard the homeward bound ships were Lt. Gen. Sir Ronald Adam and his III Corps HQ staff, their planning tasks now complete. Returning with him were the decimated remains of his command: the survivors of one regular (2nd) and two Territorial (44th and 48th) divisions.

With the departure of III Corps, Fagalde placed the depleted 21e Division d'infanterie (I/48e RI, two battalions of the 137e RI, backed up by the 35e RAD) in the line east of Bergues. The French linked with the 1st Bn. East Lancashires of the 42nd Division's 126th Brigade, which now came under command of Alexander's I Corps.

THE BIGGEST DAY, FRIDAY 31 MAY

Dover Command was greatly aided by the French navy's ad hoc 'Pas de Calais flotilla', which rescued a total of 48,474 men. Here a French minesweeper (left: two minelaying rails extending over the stern) and dispatch boat (right: one minelaying track) unload troops at Dover. (IWM HU56093)

By this time some 92,000 British and 156,000 French troops were cornered in and defiantly defending the Dunkirk perimeter. They were faced by approximately 120,000 Germans who finally came under the authority of a single commander, whose staff now began planning a coordinated series of assaults to break into the perimeter. On the western end of the line the 9. Panzer-Division launched a probing feint along the railway line between Bourbourg and Dunkirk. It was repelled by II /225e RI strongly supported by artillery (III/89e RAD). The real effort came on the eastern flank where devastating artillery barrages and three divisions attacking heavily at Bulscamp (151st Brigade), Furnes (7th Guards Brigade) and Nieuport (12th Brigade) established firm footholds on the British side of the canals. While counterattacks – supported by artillery constrained by ammunition shortages – reduced the enemy pockets, they were not eliminated.

In fact the German successes might have been greater had it not been for the only examples of Allied close air support flown for the beleaguered defenders. Just after 1600hrs, as the 256. Infanterie-Division massed its forces at a crossroads near Westende to renew attacks and exploit its bridgehead at Nieuport, ten FAA (NAS 826) Fairey Albacores (obsolete biplane replacement for the ancient Swordfish) – attacked with 250lb bombs and are credited with forestalling the impending enemy assault. They were followed four hours later by nine more modern Skuas (NAS 801) attacking German pontoon bridges across the Nieuport Canal. Jumped by Messerschmitts (3./JG 20) during egress, two Skuas were lost and a third badly damaged. Hurricanes (No. 242 Sqn.) shot down three of the attacking Bf 109Es at the cost of one of their own.

The RAF provided Lysander army cooperation aircraft (Nos. 2 and 16 Sqns.) attempting to locate German batteries bombarding the beaches and lost three of these to Messerschmitts (III./JG 26). Throughout the day 2 Group sent 93 Bristol Blenheims in small raids to bomb these and interdict troop columns moving towards Furnes from Ypres, suffering no losses.

German 10.5cm artillery, le FH 18 howitzers, find their range. Positioning his guns along the Yser River, Küchler was able to take the entire perimeter, port and beaches under intense and accurate shellfire. (IWM MH9409)

TOP
When the 2nd Bn. the Royal Ulster Rifles arrived at Bray-Dunes in the early morning hours of 1 June, they found the seas virtually empty of rescue ships. Only a stranded lifeboat, the beached paddle minesweeper *Devonia* and in the distance the burnt-out personnel ship *Crested Eagle* could be seen. (IWM HU1137)

BOTTOM
The British Army's youngest general, 48-year-old Maj. Gen. The Hon. Harold R. L. G. Alexander, DSO, was well known for his coolness under fire. Commissioned in the Irish Guards in 1911, in World War I he was wounded twice and rose quickly to command the 4th Guards Brigade. A remarkably talented officer and imperturbable leader he ensured the evacuation of the British rearguard. (IMW O1132)

Meanwhile, for most of the morning it appeared that the 248,000 Allied troops were truly trapped in the 155km² (60-square-mile) beachhead. The dawn brought an increasing onshore wind (force 3 strength) that generated a rising surf in the long shallows shelving the evacuation beaches. Scores of the small boats working the beaches broached, capsized and were pushed hard aground, and as the tide fell they were all left stranded and useless – embarkations came to a halt. Additionally German artillery had found their range on Dunkirk harbour and made daytime embarkations there very hazardous. These conditions in turn exposed the nine personnel and three hospital ships waiting offshore to increased risk of air attack. Consequently, shortly after 0700hrs Ramsay suspended dispatching additional large ships until these had returned.

During the night, Kapitänleutnant Heinz Birnbacher's 1. S-Bootsflotilla had been at work. At 0121hrs, between Westhinder and T Buoys, the 1,298-ton French destroyer *Cyclone*, limited by engine trouble to only 16 knots, was attacked by *S.24* (Oberleutnant zur See Detlefsen) and torpedoed in the bows. Badly damaged, the ship struggled back to Dover at one-quarter of its original speed, escorted by two other French vessels. (Laid up at Brest for repairs, *Cyclone* was destroyed in dry dock to prevent capture.)

Only 20 minutes later her sister ship, *Siroco*, passed T Buoy on the way to Dover with 770 troops (mostly from 16e RAD) and the colours of the 92e RI (from the 25e Division d'infanterie motorisée – smuggled out of Lille before the French surrender). Hearing aircraft overhead Capitaine Gui de Toulouse-Lautrec-Montfa slowed from 14 to 7 knots to reduce the size of his phosphorescent wake. At that moment *Siroco* was attacked by *S.23* (Oberleutnant zur See Christiansen) and *S.26* (Oberleutnant zur See Fimmen), two torpedoes hitting the stern. Shortly thereafter she capsized and sank with the loss of 59 crewmen and over 600 troops, 252 survivors being picked up by a Polish destroyer, patrol sloop *Widgeon* and two coasters.

Additionally the only Luftwaffe raid on the harbour sank the French 2,508-ton steamer *Ain el Turk*, a tug and two trawlers. However, these losses did not deter the French Navy, which organized over 30 vessels – including two other cargo ships, three warships, 11 fishing vessels and 15 Belgian trawlers – in a continuous flow, retrieving most of the 14,784 *poilus* rescued that day, including Gén. Blanchard and his staff (aboard the 669-ton torpedo boat *Bouclier*).

DAY OF THE DEFIANTS, 31 MAY 1940 (pp. 66–67)

Conceived in 1935 as the replacement for the Hawker Demon, the Boulton Paul Defiant was not intended to be a 'fighter'. Instead it was designed as a 'bomber destroyer' – intended to engage only enemy bombers while its contemporary, the Hawker Hurricane, fended off escorting fighters.

Mounting a Boulton Paul-built version of the French de Boysson four-gun turret and with no fixed forward-firing armament Defiant pilots were trained to close with enemy bomber formations from the flank, or by flying across their noses slightly below the bomber's level, in what was known as a 'crossover' attack. In this way the turret gunner would turn to fire 'broadside' against the enemy much like an ancient sailing man-of-war. The initial attack was to be concentrated on the lead bomber, thereby disrupting the defensive cohesion of the enemy formation.

At 1840hrs Squadron Leader Philip A. Hunter led a dozen Defiants to Dunkirk having coordinated with Hurricanes of No. 111 Sqn. to have them in close cover/line astern with Spitfires from No. 609 Sqn. shadowing to one side and above. Soon three of the faster Spitfires dived on a large formation of Heinkel bombers, claiming one shot down, while Hunter climbed his formation to engage and the Hurricanes turned to occupy nearby Bf 109Es.

True to doctrine Hunter and three others closed from below on the flanks of a bomber in the leading group and 16 Browning .303in. machine guns chattered away riddling its belly. This aircraft (from Stab/KG 27) was last seen circling down towards

the sea with one engine on fire and apparently crashed offshore, it and its crew being listed as missing in action.

Hunter then moved his Defiant **(1)** to the leader of another group of bombers, the aircraft (1G+AN) **(2)** of Oberleutnant Robert Kalischewski leading the 5. Staffel formation. His gunner, Leading Aircraftman F. H. King, damaged it while other Defiants engaged the remaining Heinkels as they scattered.

Pilot Officer G. Hackwood and Leading Aircraftman Lillie found themselves beneath another and Lillie opened fire at 50m (164ft), exploding the left engine. This bomber is believed to be the machine that crashed near Saint-Folquin (between Dunkirk and Calais), killing all aboard.

Pilot Officers E. G. Barwell and J. E. M. Williams **(3)** engaged another 5. Staffel machine (1G+IN) **(4)**, riddling the underside of the pilot's cabin and reportedly it 'nosed forward and dived slowly towards the sea'. It returned to base damaged with the pilot mortally wounded.

Return fire from the belly gunner damaged Barwell's aircraft, forcing him to ditch on the way home. Return fire also damaged another Defiant, the wounded gunner baling out and the pilot returning to crash-land at Manston. Failing to return were Flight Lieutenant Nicholas G. Cooke and his gunner Corporal Albert Lippert **(5)**.

This engagement proved what Defiants could do if permitted to use their practised tactics, but at a high cost.

HMS *Vanquisher* loading troops from the east jetty at low tide using makeshift ladders. Note the portside lifeboat has been disembarked and the paltry anti-aircraft armament of a single 2-pdr QF Mk II (amidships behind the searchlight platform) and a machine gun on the bridge wings. (IWM HU1153)

Once the morning haze gave way to fair, though cloudy skies the Luftwaffe returned. After noon the Germans attacked in three major waves with 195 bomber sorties, protected by 260 Messerschmitts. They were challenged by 289 RAF fighters flying in eight large (three to four squadrons) missions. These patrols were present when the three major raids arrived – at 1415hrs, 1700hrs and 1900hrs – but they failed to impede significantly the attacks, shooting down only six bombers (from KG 4 and 27, and LG 1) and four escorting Bf 109Es (III./JG 26). Conversely, return fire and Messerschmitts brought down six Spitfires, eight Hurricanes and five Defiants in these battles, the highest daily loss of the campaign.

The raids were designed to support the ground assaults and supplement artillery bombardments, concentrating attacks on the masses of British troops on and near the beaches. None of the highly effective Junkers dive-bombers were used. Richthofen's VIII Fliegerkorps stood down because its commander thought that preparations for *Fall Rot* should take priority, while the ship-sinking aces of I./KG 30 were transferred to Norway to deal with the increased Allied shipping associated with the impending assaults on German mountain troops trapped at Narvik.

Realignment of German forces attacking the Dunkirk Perimeter, 1800hrs 31 May

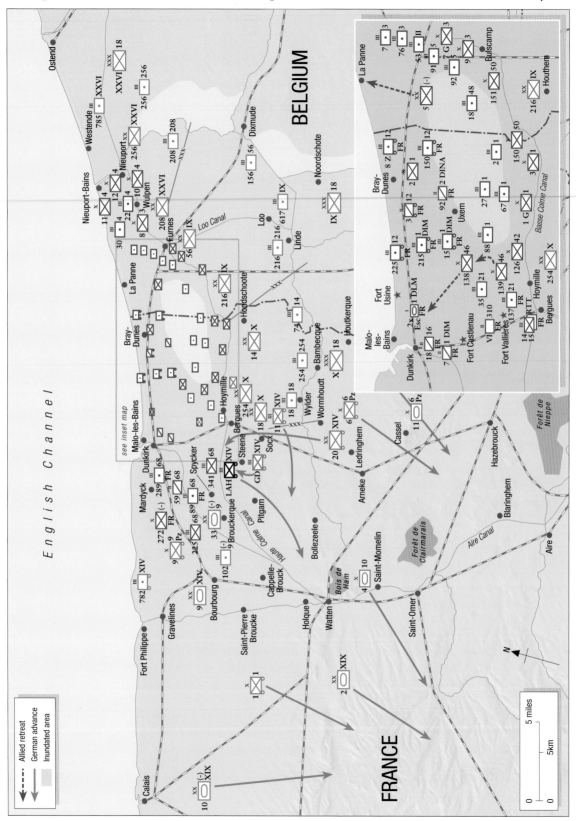

On land, Gen. Georg von Küchler attacked his new task with vigour and proved his skill as an artillerist. Arraying his corps' and divisions' 10.5cm and 15.5cm guns along the Yser River he took the harbour and the entire beach under tremendous fire. Assured of air superiority, he even used two World War I observation balloons to adjust the fall of shot! His large guns were placed so close they damaged the destroyer HMS *Vivacious* (off Bray-Dunes) with two hits, killing three and wounding 12 aboard.

By midday the wind had abated and almost all the British personnel ships had returned and at 1300hrs Ramsay ordered his recently organized armada of 'little ships' gathered at Ramsgate to sail across to Dunkirk. This ragtag regatta sailed via Route X at a stately 6 knots, over 100 boats and barges being towed by a miscellany of tugs, yachts, drifters and *schyuts*, some of them in chains up to 12 boats long. Six Tilbury tugs towed 46 lifeboats taken from ocean liners docked in London. Another brought four RAF seaplane tender motorboats and an army motor craft. Nine more pulled 17 (some provision-laden) barges from Gravesend. The SVP's Sheerness Division contributed five motorized (Dutch and Belgian) 'X lighters', a tug and a *schuyt* towing 23 motorboats; Yarmouth Base sent 13 of the 19 drifters; Portsmouth Inner Patrol provided nine of the 16 yachts. Seven fast War Department launches, six Thames Estuary 'cockle' (fishing) boats, six slow hopper barges and four 'motor coasters' were also among the continuous stream that stretched 8km (5 miles) and began arriving off the beaches from 1900hrs onwards.

Initially the arriving hosts of small ships and boats were in considerable disarray, tending to stop at the first place they came to where other craft were assembled (off Malo-les-Bains and Bray-Dunes). The artillery barrages deterred many from moving on to their assigned beaches near La Panne and in fact the shellfire drove off a number of small boats, their untrained and undisciplined civilian crews fleeing from the frightening bombardment. Vice Admiral Ramsay ordered the captain of one minesweeper to 'arrest any little ship returning empty', a singularly impossible task.

Ironically, even though they were the only Ju 87 crews specifically trained in anti-ship attacks I.(Stuka)/Trägergruppe (Carrier Group) 186 – seen here during a pre-war training mission – was the last to join VIII Fliegerkorps. Attached to StG 1, they formed part of the awesome 'cloud of Stukas' that rained destruction upon the Allied evacuation fleet off the beaches. (IWM HU103326)

A target-rich environment: a host of shipping waits offshore at La Panne, being overflown by a Coastal Command Lockheed Hudson. 1 June dawned a bright and clear day, perfect weather for Stuka attacks. One destroyer heads outbound while a minesweeper, destroyer and large tug – none of which survived the morning – steam towards the crowd of *schuyts*, trawlers and drifters nearer the water's edge. (IWM C1715)

At 1800hrs the BEF GHQ closed down and evacuated King Albert's old seaside villa, most of the staff being ferried out to the destroyer HMS *Keith*. Lord Gort was initially brought to the modern 830-ton minesweeper *Hebe* where he observed the progress of the evacuation at Bray-Dunes for six hours before a motor anti-submarine boat sped him to Dover, arriving at 0547hrs.

At 2300hrs the withdrawal of II Corps began, organized and led by Maj. Gen. Montgomery (Lt. Gen. Brooke and his staff had left the previous day). Montgomery's 3rd Division and Maj. Gen. Franklyn's badly battered 5th Division got away safely from Bray-Dunes, but Major-General Dudley Johnson's 4th Division had problems. Planned to depart from La Panne, few ships appeared offshore and by 0100hrs only 300–400 of Johnson's 8,000 men had been embarked. Moving to Bray-Dunes they were unable to embark largely because the Royal Navy shore parties – who had been directed that they 'were not to risk being taken prisoner' – were convinced by the bombardments that the enemy was closing in so they re-embarked and all returned to England by 0830hrs the next morning. After a 16km march to the east mole, the tired Tommies were finally able to board the ships berthed there.

In spite of all adversity some 53,230 British troops evacuated on this, the biggest day of *Dynamo*. Almost two-thirds of the total left from the harbour and of that number approximately 1,176 were wounded. Ship losses were light: two motorboats due to enemy action and two ALCs and ten motorboats lost by misadventure. Four destroyers were damaged in accidents but the only major Royal Navy loss was a damaged 622-ton paddle-wheel minesweeper that was intentionally beached near Bray-Dunes to form a breakwater for the smaller boats.

Général Fagalde anticipated II Corps' retirement and positioned Général de brigade Louis Janssen's still strong 12e Division d'infanterie motorisée along the Canal des Chats and the frontier line – a series of widely spaced bunkers that dotted the Belgian border. Major-General Martel's small but still effective 50th Division pulled back to Bray-Dunes to become I Corps' reserve behind Janssen's 8e RZ manning the frontier line.

Command of the last remaining British corps was passed to Maj. Gen. Alexander, who replaced the overage (a Boer War veteran), utterly exhausted and chronically ineffectual Lieutenant-General Michael G. H. Barker. Alexander's front line consisted of six battalions; defending Bergues was the 477-man 1st Bn. The Loyal Regiment (known as 'the Loyals') from his division's 2nd Brigade. Along the Basse Colme Canal were two battalions from the 126th Brigade (now attached to the 46th Division), the 2nd Bn. The Coldstream Guards (1st Guards Brigade) and 1st Bn. Duke of Wellingtons (3rd Brigade). A large detachment from the 2nd Bn. The Sherwood Foresters (also 3rd Brigade) manned the three concrete bunkers studding the Belgian border, spanning the 3.2km (2 miles) across Les Moëres inundation.

THE LUFTWAFFE'S LAST CHANCE, SATURDAY 1 JUNE

Finally learning that the prey was getting away and that his boasts would likely return empty Göring, who had been touring Dutch cities confiscating loot for his collections, rushed back to work in an attempt to re-energize his commanders and reverse the Luftwaffe's impending failure to fulfil his vainglorious promises.

With clear skies to work in, the Luftwaffe struck ferociously, attacking with 160 bomber and 325 Stuka sorties, the largest numbers used during the whole campaign. Arriving in five major raids they were met by the RAF's typical defensive response: 267 fighter sorties flown in eight missions. However there were long gaps between them, resulting in little opposition, and even when the RAF was present the 420 Bf 109Es and 110 Bf 110s successfully protected their charges – only two bombers (1./KG 4 and 4./KG 76) and two Stukas (I.(St)/TrGr 186) were lost to RAF fighters while six Hurricanes and ten Spitfires were shot down. The Luftwaffe lost seven Bf 109Es and three Bf 110Cs.

Consequently, diving out of clear blue skies, the heavy air assaults wreaked havoc amongst the evacuation fleet. Attacks began at 0415hrs when a formation of 40 Stukas (StG 1) arrived before 11 Group's 'dawn patrol' and attacked ships offshore, followed about three hours later (0720hrs) by an even larger raid (StG 2 and 77 accompanied by Ju 88s from LG 1). By the time the RAF's next patrol arrived at 0900hrs the dive-bombers had sunk three destroyers, one minesweeper and two large naval tugs.

The primary target off Bray-Dunes was the large (1,400-ton) destroyer HMS *Keith*, flagship of both R. Adm. Wake-Walker and Captain Edward L. Berthon, commander of Dover's 19th Destroyer Flotilla. Down to only 30 rounds of anti-aircraft ammo by daybreak she was soon defenceless, overwhelmed and bombed by all three waves, finally capsizing with 36 dead aboard. The destroyers *Basilisk* and *Havant* were also hit (another 42 killed) and later sank or were scuttled. The destroyer *Ivanhoe* was hit amidships (26 killed/30 wounded) and had to be towed back to Dover, out of action for almost three months. The modern minesweeper *Skipjack* was hit by five bombs, sinking immediately with 275 troops trapped below decks. The large 550-ton Admiralty tug *St Abbs*, having rescued many of the *Keith*'s survivors, was blown out of the water by a single bomb from a Ju 88, killing 105.

At 1000hrs the carnage continued as Dorniers (KG 76) and Heinkels (KG 4) rained sticks of bombs on the huge collection of vessels. The 585-ton HMS *Mosquito* (built as a Yangtze River gunboat, now a part of the Thames Estuary Defence Flotilla) was hit, set on fire and abandoned, later scuttled by sister ship *Locust*. The 4,240-ton railway steamer *Prague* was returning with 3,000 French troops aboard when it was badly damaged at 1009hrs. Sinking by the stern but able to maintain some speed, *Prague* transferred the troops while still under way, passing them to a destroyer and two minesweepers. The steamer eventually beached off Deal.

Not needed to fend off the RAF, during the morning Luftwaffe fighters destroyed two Lysanders (Nos. 2 and 26 Sqns.) and shot down a pair of Coastal Command Blenheim light bombers (No. 254 Sqn.) whose pilots made the unwise decision to try intercepting German bomber formations. The only loss was a Bf 109E (1./JG 20) surprised by an 'upgunned' Avro Anson (No. 500 Sqn.), which recently had additional .303in. Browning machine guns mounted in its side windows.

German heavy artillery, 17cm K 18 and 21cm Mrs 18 (shown here), at Nieuport and between Gravelines and Mardyke finally shut down the Royal Navy's daytime evacuations from Dunkirk and the beaches. (IWM MH9200)

German fighters failed to prevent the French Aéronavale from flying an interdiction mission on behalf of the beleaguered defenders. Staging through RAF Tangmere the night before, six American-made Vought 156Fs of Escadrille AB 1 attacked enemy troops at Furnes, now well behind the lines. The French pilots all eluded Luftwaffe fighters and survived the flak, four returning to their base at Cherbourg, the other pair landing in England for the night.

Four squadrons of Hurricanes (Nos. 43, 145, 245 and 609 Sqns.) were overhead at 1030hrs when the Stukas returned, but escorting Bf 109Es (II./JG 26) kept them at bay (shooting down five for the loss of two) while the Junkers attacked the arriving 1,356-ton French destroyer *Foudroyant* (Capitaine de corvette Pierre Fontaine) and two returning British ships.

Trapped in the narrow channel of Route X where manoeuvring was impossible, *Foudroyant* was 'submerged in a cloud of Stukas'. Shattered by three direct hits and numerous near misses, the large French destroyer quickly capsized and sank. A French auxiliary minesweeper, tug, two trawlers and a motor yacht rescued 157 crewmen.

The old 3,454-ton railway steamer *Scotia* and the ancient 519-ton British paddle-wheel minesweeper *Brighton Queen* were returning via Route X with 2,700 French troops aboard and just beyond Mardyck were attacked by a dozen bombers. *Scotia* quickly took three devastating hits aft and began sinking and heeling to starboard. *Brighton Queen* was also hit and began sinking. A destroyer, minesweeper and three drifters rescued about 2,000 survivors.

Finally, at 1600hrs the last raid – by nine Stukas – caught a flotilla of four small (300-ton) French auxiliary minesweepers headed for the harbour and sank three of them.

While thickening clouds inhibited further air attacks, Küchler's big guns came into play even more against the evacuation fleet. Positioning some of his 15.5cm and 21cm artillery (Artillerie-Regiment 782) just inshore of the beach at les Huttes and le Clipon; they sank a 96-ton drifter and hit two ships in the harbour.

Victoria Cross recipient Captain Harold Marcus Ervine-Andrews, commander of B Company, 1st Bn. the East Lancashire Regiment. His heroic and successful 'last stand' at the Bentie-Meulen Bridge permitted the rest of the battalion to withdraw and evacuate. (IWM HU2611)

The Kriegsmarine also took their toll on the Allied shipping. Early in the morning, Kapitänleutnant Rudolf Petersen's 2. S-Bootsflotilla was out hunting once again and near South Falls shoals HMS *Widgeon* was attacked and missed. *S.35* (Oberleutnant zur See Keecke) sank one 550-ton anti-submarine trawler near T Buoy at 0230hrs and twenty minutes later *S.34* (Oberleutnant zur See Obermaier) sank another (of 540 tons) near S Buoy.

On the ground Küchler's troops began their last stage of coordinated assaults designed to crack open the perimeter. On the eastern front XXVI AK (256. and 208. Infanterie-Divisionen) awoke to find that the British units defending Nieuport had vanished in the night. The void was filled by General der Infanterie Hermann Geyer's IX AK (56. and 216. Infanterie-Divisionen), which spent the day advancing to the frontier line. In the west the 9. Panzer-Division made some desultory attacks against the well dug-in French 68e Division d'infanterie, but these were mostly designed to occupy Beaufrère's infantry and artillery and prevent them from supporting the defenders along the southern sector. There Küchler planned for Generalleutnant Christian Hansen's X AK to split the perimeter at the seam between the French and British forces, rolling each side back to the flank and advancing from Bergues to Dunkirk.

Under devastatingly heavy artillery barrages the ferocious German ground assaults began at 0500hrs. Tremendous bombardments on Bergues destroyed the town and drove the Loyals across the canal to the north, leaving the 1,000-man 14e and 15e RRT holding the blazing ruins. In heavy fighting around Hoymille the 18. Infanterie-Division stormed the Basse Colme Canal, driving back a company of Royal Warwickshires and turning the flank of the neighbouring French I/137e RI. Late afternoon counterattacks by the Loyals – slogging through flooded fields in the face of withering machine-gun fire – eventually stabilized the line along the canal bank.

Five kilometres (3 miles) east of Bergues the 254. Infanterie-Division's assaults forced the two battalions of the 126th Brigade from their forward positions. They retired under vicious fire to the Canal des Chats, one of them covered by Captain Harold M. Ervine-Andrews and his company of only 40 men – winning the Victoria Cross for his valiant leadership. (Only he and eight men survived the desperate last-ditch battle unscathed.)

While German attacks breached the Basse Colme Canal line at several points, nightfall and exhaustion prevented exploiting the penetrations. As the fighting died down and darkness enveloped the scene British troops all along the Les Moëres salient withdrew through the French units lining the Canal des Chats; their job was done. The battered troops moved wearily to Dunkirk and Malo-les-Bains where they queued up for evacuation, becoming the last of some 64,429 men rescued that day. Over half – some 35,013 – were French troops, many of them (for the first time) carried by vessels of the Royal Navy.

Of the total, 2,509 were wounded. This would be the last of the seriously wounded rescued because at 1400hrs Capt. Tennant made the difficult decision to discontinue embarking stretcher cases, except aboard dedicated hospital carriers. A stretcher occupied the same deck space as eight soldiers standing/four men sitting and England's immediate need was for able-bodied troops. With great sadness an estimated 1,200 wounded (plus one medical officer and ten orderlies for each hundred) had to be abandoned to the occupying Germans.

While the rescue effort was nearly as prodigious as the previous day, it had been at tremendous cost; all told, 17 ships were lost – including four precious destroyers with two more laid up for months – and another eight seriously

damaged. The RAF had proved incapable of preventing the Luftwaffe's heavy attacks and the shore batteries now commanded all routes into Dunkirk as well as the harbour and waters off the beaches. The evacuation was now untenable during daylight hours and at 1800hrs Tennant, who had witnessed the carnage from atop the large French HQ bunker (Bastion 32), signalled Ramsay 'Things are getting very hot for ships… Have directed that no ships sail during daylight. Evacuation by transports therefore ceases at 0300.' Vice Admiral Dover – and the Admiralty for that matter – had of course come to the same conclusion. Just as the 'night shift' of evacuation vessels (seven destroyers and four personnel ships to serve the harbour and 11 minesweepers and a few *schuyts*, drifters and small craft to work off Malo-les-Bains) began sailing from England – Ramsay ordered all ships to withdraw from Dunkirk before sunrise.

While the British accounting of embarkations ended with tallying the day's debarkations at midnight, the evacuation continued through the night. Boarding the ships were most of the 1st Division, the 46th Division's 126th and 139th Brigades, and I Corps artillery and support units.

As ordered, at 0300hrs the last two vessels – the destroyers *Whitshed* and *Winchelsea* – pulled up their gangplanks and boarding ladders, cast off and backed out of the harbour, leaving the east mole jetty crowded with troops. The Tommies were the grim and grimy survivors of the Loyals, bone-tired from the 8km (5-mile) trek from Bergues that followed a day of non-stop bombardment and combat.

Dejected, yet accepting that the evacuation was suspended for the coming day, they 'about-faced' and marched from the mole and into the dunes beyond Malo-les-Bains. There the Loyals joined about 3,500 other troops forming a last redoubt around the last portal, just in case the French collapsed during the day. Defended by a dozen 2-pdr anti-tank guns and seven Bofors, they dug in deep in the sandy dunes and waited for the day to pass and the Royal Navy to return.

THE FRENCH FIGHT ON, SUNDAY 2 JUNE

As the sun rose again the millpond-smooth seas off Dunkirk were almost empty, only HMS *Calcutta* and two sloops, and two patrols of anti-submarine trawlers guarding Route Y – and a host of wrecks along the beaches – remained.

The RAF initiated the day's air activity. Covered by a four-squadron patrol, seven Lysanders located German artillery, including the two shore batteries, unmolested. Covered by another four fighter squadrons, 24 Blenheims bombed the big guns, losing three bombers (No. 107 Sqn.) to German flak.

The first Luftwaffe raid – Heinkels from KG 54 and Stukas from StG 2 – arrived at 0800hrs protected by fighters from four Bf 109E (JG 26 plus I./JG 27) and one Bf 110C *Gruppen* (II./ZG 26). The 120 German aircraft were met by five RAF squadrons (Nos. 32, 66, 92, 266 and 611 Sqns.) and a fierce air battle ensued. The Messerschmitts again prevailed, shooting down five Spitfires and one Hurricane for the loss of a single Bf 109E (3./JG 27). Flight Lieutenant R. R. Stanford Tuck (later a hero of the Battle of Britain) led No. 92 Sqn. through the mêlée, 'sighted and attacked eight Heinkel 111[s]. Shot down one and was attacked by six 109[s]…' No. 92 Sqn. destroyed six bombers for no loss, only Tuck's Spitfire damaged. No. 611 Sqn. accounted for the single Ju 87B (1./StG 2) shot down, but were mauled by the Messerschmitts losing two Spitfires shot down (pilots killed in action) and six damaged (pilots unhurt).

The Allies also initiated the ground fighting. At 0600hrs the 550-man 21e Centre d'instruction divisionnaire launched a vigorous counterattack against the German bridgehead east of Hoymille, sloshing through thigh-deep water and being scythed down by machine-gun fire. Aided by two reconnaissance groups and six Somua S35 tanks, within three hours the French recaptured Notre Dame des Neiges, but only 65 men survived unscathed. Unable to hold the ground regained, they withdrew to Canal des Moëres.

British Tommies about to step onto home soil once again, and very happy to do so. (IWM H1628)

German attacks did not resume until the afternoon when at 1500hrs the newly arrived 61. Infanterie-Division (from AOK 6's IV AK) – advancing behind PzKpfw III and IV medium tanks from 3. and 6./PR 33 (9. Panzer-Division) – attacked along the main road to Spycker. French infantry (I/225e RI) fought stubbornly and 75mm gunners (III/35e RAD) fired over open sights for three hours before they were finally overrun. The Germans advanced only as far as Spycker before the fighting ended at 2300hrs.

On the eastern end of the perimeter the 56. Infanterie-Division attacked the frontier line, but was repulsed with heavy losses. Stuka attacks attempted to aid a breakthrough, bombing the 12e Division d'infanterie motorisée HQ in Fort Usine and killing Gén. Janssen. Stiff defence (8e RZ) held the Germans and spirited counterattacks (by 150e RI) netted 60 prisoners. In the evening the 56. Infanterie-Division pulled out and marched south, its place filled by the 208. Infanterie-Division.

Küchler's main effort remained in the centre where the 18. Infanterie-Division resumed their attacks at Bergues at 1500hrs with a 15-minute bombardment by Stukas, immediately followed by specially trained shock troops (Pion. Bat. 18) charging through great gaps blown in the

ancient Vauban walls. The dazed survivors of the two RTT battalions were overwhelmed, surrendered or scattered northwards. Meanwhile another 24 Stukas attacked Fort Vallières, killing most of the garrison (VI/310e RI). The Germans advanced against determined resistance until a desperate counterattack halted them short of the Canal des Moëres.

The Luftwaffe returned to attack ships offshore, three Ju 88As damaging the anti-aircraft cruiser *Calcutta* with near misses at 1035hrs, forcing her retirement to Sheerness four hours later. About that time another dozen Junkers caught the 2,294-ton hospital carrier *Worthing* approaching Dunkirk and damaged her with two near misses; she withdrew as well. One 399-ton anti-submarine trawler was also badly damaged and retired; two others were lost to mines.

The RAF finally returned near dusk to cover the approach of the evacuation fleet. At 2010hrs the four squadrons met a large formation of Dorniers, Stukas and Messerschmitts. One Hurricane (No. 111 Sqn.) was lost while three Ju 87s (III./StG 2) were destroyed. The Germans attacked the 1,790-ton hospital carrier *Paris* (sent to replace the *Worthing*), the 2,060-ton *Royal Daffodil* and a pair of RAF seaplane tender motorboats, all approaching Dunkirk. The *Paris* was attacked by an estimated 15 bombers, who killed two crewmen and damaged the ship so badly that it withdrew and sank the next day. (Consequently, only 167 wounded, all ambulatory, were evacuated this day.) One of the RAF motorboats (No. 243) was sunk by four Ju 87s and many of the night's Royal Naval pier party were killed. The *Royal Daffodil* was attacked by another half-dozen and damaged with a direct hit that went through the hull. She returned to Margate in a sinking condition.

At 2100hrs, after the Luftwaffe had retired for the evening, Ramsay's last batch of evacuation vessels – 11 destroyers, eight personnel ships (others were ordered, three failed to comply), 14 minesweepers, nine drifters, six *schuyts*, two armed yachts, one gunboat and three tugs towing small craft – began to arrive. Almost matching this long, strung-out, slow-moving convoy was the French effort of 43 ships, including the large destroyer *Léopard*, two torpedo boats, six smaller warships and 34 French and Belgian fishing vessels.

By midnight these ships had rescued 7,208 British troops, the last of which – the 3rd Brigade's 1st Bn. The King's Shropshire Light Infantry – boarded the 1,952-ton *St. Helier* and departed at 2330hrs, allowing Capt. Tennant to announce to V. Adm. Ramsay: 'Operation complete. Returning to Dover', which was reworded for posterity as 'BEF evacuated'. Major-General Alexander and his staff were picked up by R. Adm. Wake-Walker in a motor anti-submarine boat and, after checking for stragglers, ferried to the destroyer *Venomous* for their return to England.

With the departure of Capt. Tennant's control team embarkations came to almost a complete halt – the French did not have a comparable capability. German shellfire precluded lifting troops from Malo-les-Bains and a complicated assortment of miscommunications amongst the Allies resulted in most French troops not arriving on Jetée de l'est until 0230hrs. With orders to depart promptly at 0300hrs, five destroyers and a personnel ship returned virtually empty, leaving an estimated 10,000 Frenchmen behind.

THE BRITISH ARE GONE, 3 AND 4 JUNE

The night's debacle left Fagalde with 25,000 troops manning the shrunken perimeter and another 22,000 ready for embarkation. It was guessed that 20,000 men more were present but unaccounted for, bunched in thousands of tiny groups cloistered in cellars and cowering in the dunes. Unfortunately, this was to prove a low estimate.

Again Fagalde hoped to upset the Germans' planned assaults with a pre-emptive spoiling attack. At 0400hrs four battalions – two from Général de division M. C. Gabriel Lucas's 32e Division d'infanterie (III/122e RI and III/143e RI) and two from the 137e RI – supported by their last (six S35 and four H35) tanks. The exhausted *poilus* were able to push as far as Galghouck before enemy anti-tank gunners knocked out the tanks and machine guns stopped the assault.

While the 61. Infanterie-Division and the refreshed 208. Infanterie-Division renewed their assaults – and made progress – on the flanks of the perimeter earlier that morning, the Germans' main effort was again in the centre. At 1100hrs Gen.Lt. Friedrich-Carl Cranz's 18. Infanterie-Division launched their attacks, supported by heavy artillery bombardments, driving the French back to Canal des Moëres. Of the I/137e RI – a unit that had been in the forefront of the fighting ever since it battled Guderian's Panzers at Bourbourg – only 50 men remained.

Meanwhile, haze and heavy ground mist hampered RAF operations over Dunkirk but there was little enemy air activity anyway, the Luftwaffe stood down most units to prepare for Operation *Paula*, the massive afternoon offensive (640 bombers escorted by 460 Messerschmitts) against Armée de l'Air bases and French aviation industry targets around Paris. In the one rare encounter, No. 17 Sqn. lost one Hurricane to Bf 109Es (5./JG 3) for no victories.

The Dutch *schuyt Oranje* unloading troops at Ramsgate. Manned by Royal Naval crews the 40 *schuyts* performed yeoman service in the evacuation, recovering 22,698 men and losing only four of their number in the entire operation. (IWM HU1518)

Knowing the night's evacuations would be the final effort overruled the chronic fatigue being suffered by all the crews – Royal Navy, merchant navy and civilian alike – so Ramsay sent everything available: all nine surviving destroyers, nine personnel ships (a tenth refused to go), eleven minesweepers, two patrol sloops and one gunboat, plus nine drifters, five *schuyts* and four tugs towing 14 motorboats. To bring off as many of their countrymen as possible, the French provided 63 vessels – including four destroyers, eight smaller warships, 18 trawlers and a host of fishing boats. Being slower, the small craft departed first, beginning at 1430hrs, followed two hours later by the tugs and *schuyts* and their chains of small boats. At 1815–1845hrs the British and French cross-Channel steamers departed, with the destroyers and other naval vessels after them. His flag flying from Motor Torpedo Boat *102*, R. Adm. Wake-Walker left with the destroyers, minesweepers, sloops and gunboat. To aid in controlling the flow of troops, the Royal Navy provided a pier party under Commander Herbert James Buchanan with 54 Royal Navy personnel and four French liaison officers to assist in overcoming language difficulties.

Anticipating the ships' arrival, at 1900hrs HQ Forces Maritimes du Nord shut down operations and an hour later left Bastion 32 for the Jetée de l'est. Most of them boarded the British car ferry *Autocarrier* and French *Newhaven* and were gone by midnight. Two hours later Vice-amiral Abrial and Gén. Fagalde boarded two French motor torpedo boats and headed for Dover.

At 2030hrs Gén. Barthélemy's troops began slipping out of line, leaving skirmishers who would remain until 0200hrs, only the depleted battalions holding the bridges at Chapeau Rouge (II/48e, III/122e and II/137e RI) being unable to disengage. However, as his ragged, weary warriors tramped towards Malo-les-Bains, 'a vast crowd of troops materialise[d]… out of the cellars and holes streams of unarmed men appeared, emerging everywhere, converging on the Mole, until they became an immense river of men frozen almost solid at its approaches'. These were ordnance troops, transport drivers and other auxiliary

GERMAN FORCES

A XIV Armeekorps (mot.) heavy artillery batteries
B Schützen-Brigade 9
C 61. Infanterie-Division
D Infanterie-Regiment 'Grossdeutschland'
E 18. Infanterie-Division
F 254. Infanterie-Division
G 14. Infanterie-Division
H 216. Infanterie-Division
I 56. Infanterie-Division
J 208. Infanterie-Division
K IX Armeekorps heavy artillery batteries
L 256. Infanterie-Division

FMN

ABRIAL

ROU

ZU

FORT USINE

MALO-LES-BAINS

DUNKIRK EAST MOLE

DUNKIRK WEST MOLE 12

11

5

25

10 20

16

24

21

DUNKIRK OIL REFINERY

15

14

10

11

FORT CASTELNAU

SAINT-POL-SUR-MER

ROUTE X

2

2

6

FORT VALLIÈ

1

2

6

7

A

4

7

3

4

4

5

B

2

6

BOURBOURG CANAL

BOURBOURG

C

ALLIED FORCES
French
1 272e Demi-brigade d'infanterie
2 59e GRDI
3 II/225e Régiment d'infanterie
4 III/341e Régiment d'infanterie
5 III/35e Regiment d'artillerie
6 I/225e Régiment d'infanterie
7 341e Régiment d'infanterie
8 14e and 15e Régiments régionaux de
   travailleurs
9 I/48e Régiment d'infanterie and Usherforce
10 7e GRDA
11 18e GRCA
12 21e Centre d'instruction divisionnaire
13 VI/310e Régiment d'infanterie
14 III/407e Régiment d'infanterie
15 III/225e Régiment d'infanterie
16 137e Régiment d'infanterie
17 III/122e Régiment d'infanterie
18 III/143e Régiment d'infanterie
19 92e GRDI
20 3e GRDI
21 150e Régiment d'infanterie
22 8e Régiment de zouaves
23 12e Division d'infanterie motorisée HQ
24 Forces Maritimes du Nord and 16e Corps
   d'armée HQ at Bastion 32

British
25 Remaining troops of the 1st Division

AA CANAL

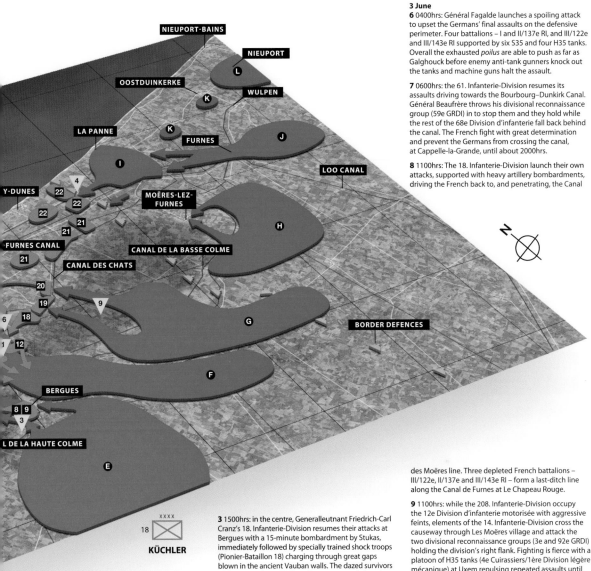

3 June

6 0400hrs: Général Fagalde launches a spoiling attack to upset the Germans' final assaults on the defensive perimeter. Four battalions – I and II/137e RI, and III/122e and III/143e RI supported by six S35 and four H35 tanks. Overall the exhausted *poilus* are able to push as far as Galghouck before enemy anti-tank gunners knock out the tanks and machine guns halt the assault.

7 0600hrs: the 61. Infanterie-Division resumes its assaults driving towards the Bourbourg–Dunkirk Canal. Général Beaufrère throws his divisional reconnaissance group (59e GRDI) in to stop them and they hold while the rest of the 68e Division d'infanterie fall back behind the canal. The French fight with great determination and prevent the Germans from crossing the canal, at Cappelle-la-Grande, until about 2000hrs.

8 1100hrs: The 18. Infanterie-Division launch their own attacks, supported with heavy artillery bombardments, driving the French back to, and penetrating, the Canal

Map labels:

NIEUPORT-BAINS
NIEUPORT
OOSTDUINKERKE
WULPEN
LA PANNE
FURNES
Y-DUNES
MOËRES-LEZ-FURNES
LOO CANAL
FURNES CANAL
CANAL DE LA BASSE COLME
CANAL DES CHATS
BORDER DEFENCES
BERGUES
L DE LA HAUTE COLME

XXXX
18
KÜCHLER

EVENTS

2 June

1 0600hrs: the 21e Centre d'instruction divisionnaire, supported by two reconnaissance groups (7e GRDI and 18e GRCA) and six Somua S35 tanks (18e Dragons/1ère DLM), launches a vigorous counterattack against the German bridgehead east of Hoymille. Against withering machine-gun fire they manage to retake Notre Dame des Neiges at 0900hrs, but are badly depleted. Unable to hold the ground regained, they withdraw to Canal des Moëres.

2 1500hrs: German attacks resume when Generalleutnant Siegfried Haenicke's newly arrived 61. Infanterie-Division – advancing behind PzKpfw III and IV medium tanks of PR 33 (9. Panzer-Division) – attack along the main road to Spycker. The I/225e RI fights stubbornly while 75mm guns (III/35e RAD), placed in the front line as anti-tank weapons, fire over open sights. After three hours of horrendous combat the French are finally overrun and the Germans advance as far as Spycker.

3 1500hrs: in the centre, Generalleutnant Friedrich-Carl Cranz's 18. Infanterie-Division resumes their attacks at Bergues with a 15-minute bombardment by Stukas, immediately followed by specially trained shock troops (Pionier-Bataillon 18) charging through great gaps blown in the ancient Vauban walls. The dazed survivors of the 14e and 15e RRT battalions are overwhelmed, the Germans capturing the ruins in two hours. Général Barthélemy blocks the German advance with two infantry battalions (III/225e and III/407e RI) and six groups of 75mm guns. A spoiling counterattack by infantry and four Hotchkiss H35 tanks (12e Dragons) stops the German advance before it reaches Canal des Moëres.

4 1500hrs: simultaneous attacks on the perimeter's east end by 56. Infanterie-Division are repulsed by 8e RZ with heavy losses. Stuka attacks attempt to aid a breakthrough, bombing the 12e Division d'infanterie motorisée HQ in Fort Usine (also known as 'fort des dunes') and killing Gén. Janssen. Spirited counterattacks by 150e RI net 60 prisoners. In the evening the 56. Infanterie-Division is replaced by the 208. Infanterie-Division.

5 2100hrs: the last remaining British troops – some 4,000 men from various 1st Division units plus about 3,000 stragglers – move from their bivouac in the dunes near Malo-les-Bains to the east mole for evacuation. The last British troops depart Dunkirk at 2330hrs.

des Moëres line. Three depleted French battalions – III/122e, II/137e and III/143e RI – form a last-ditch line along the Canal de Furnes at Le Chapeau Rouge.

9 1100hrs: while the 208. Infanterie-Division occupy the 12e Division d'infanterie motorisée with aggressive feints, elements of the 14. Infanterie-Division cross the causeway through Les Moëres village and attack the two divisional reconnaissance groups (3e and 92e GRDI) holding the division's right flank. Fighting is fierce with a platoon of H35 tanks (4e Cuirassiers/1ère Division légère mécanique) at Uxem repulsing repeated assaults until they are all knocked out. The Germans finally capture the village at 1800hrs.

10 2030hrs: except for the depleted battalions holding the bridges at Le Chapeau Rouge, who are unable to disengage, Gén. Barthélemy's troops began slipping out of line, leaving skirmishers in forward positions until 0200hrs. As the 25,000 combat troops move towards the quays and moles for embarkation, they find that some 40,000 support personnel have emerged from hiding in the cellars and dunes forming an impenetrable rabble that board the waiting ships ahead of the fighting men.

11 1900hrs: HQ Forces Maritimes du Nord shut down operations and depart from the east mole by midnight. At 0200hrs Vice-amiral Abrial and Gén. Fagalde board two French motor torpedo boats and depart.

12 0340hrs: the last *Dynamo* evacuation ship, HMS *Shikari* embarks 383 French troops, including Gén. Barthélemy. Simultaneously the 687-ton *Pacifico* is scuttled, temporarily blocking Dunkirk harbour.

DEFENDING THE DUNKIRK PERIMETER, 2–4 JUNE 1940

The contracted Dunkirk defensive perimeter as it was defended on 2–4 June 1940, after the departure of the last major British units.

A small portion of the estimated 40,000 French POWs captured at Dunkirk. (IWM MH2396)

personnel who for days had been cowering in the rubble and the dunes and they numbered an estimated 40,000, an undisciplined mob pushing themselves ahead of the rearguard and crowding onto the east mole to be embarked. To French historian Jacques Mordal (quoted above), 'No episode in the epic of Dunkirk caused more heartbreak.'

German shellfire was not a factor this last night – their troops were too close to risk it – but the glut of vessels crowding into Dunkirk harbour created an extreme collision hazard, one trawler being sunk and two naval vessels badly damaged. Additionally at the west mole the World War I minesweeper *Kellet* ran aground in the darkness and was so badly damaged she could embark only 30 troops. Even the flat-bottomed, 452-ton *schuyt Lena* grounded in the mud and had to be abandoned.

At the end of the east mole, once the initial congestion was resolved the personnel ships docked and loaded first, although the strong wind and fast tides resulted in slower manoeuvring and longer stays dockside. They departed followed by the minesweepers, *schuyts*, trawlers and drifters, accompanied by the last of the Belgian tugs, the crews of the four lost being carried to Dover by the *Goliath*. Finally the destroyers warped alongside the east mole for their last loads. At 0318hrs the destroyer *Express* backed out of the harbour with 611 troops and the Royal Naval pier party aboard, completing her sixth run back to England.

Trying to make up for a failed attempt the previous morning, at about 0300hrs two blockships approached the harbour entrance, escorted by the old destroyer *Shikari*, MTB *107* and MA/SB *10*. HMS *Shikari* moved to the east mole where she embarked 383 French troops, including Gén. Barthélemy. As *Shikari* backed out of the harbour at 0340hrs, Lieutenant-Commander G. H. F. Owles fired the charges that sank the 687-ton *Pacifico*, successfully – though only temporarily – closing Dunkirk harbour.

The last shipping loss of Operation *Dynamo* occurred at 0615hrs when the 348-ton French auxiliary minesweeper *Emil Deschamps*, carrying 817 troops, hit a mine only 8km (5 miles) east of Foreness. The 801-ton steamer *King George V* and the 710-ton minesweeper *Albury* rescued 107 survivors.

During 3 June and the night that followed, some 46,792 French (and six British stragglers) were evacuated to England, a tremendously successful effort in spite of all the problems both ashore and afloat. Unfortunately another 40,000 – almost all of Beaufrère's valiant rearguard – remained.

German ground assaults on the reduced perimeter resumed at dawn, but by this point the defenders realized continued resistance was futile and white flags began appearing everywhere. The 18. Infanterie-Division quickly crossed the Canal des Moëres and into the devastated city, advanced elements riding in trucks drove all the way to the base of the east mole arriving at 0930hrs to find so many French troops massed there it was difficult to round them up quickly.

Shortly before ten o'clock Gen.Lt. Cranz drove up to the red brick Hôtel de Ville, Gén. Beaufrère's final HQ, in the centre of the debris-clogged city. The French commander traded his steel helmet for the gold-leaf general's kepi for the surrender ceremony. Accepting the French capitulation, Cranz asked, 'Where are the English?' 'Not here,' Beaufrère answered, 'They are in England.'

AFTERMATH

I felt that, however the situation might develop valuable cadres had been withdrawn which would enable the fighting units of the BEF to be quickly reformed at home.
General the Viscount Gort Report to the War Cabinet, 1 June 1940

By any measure Operation *Dynamo* was a huge success as a naval evacuation. Royal Naval sources say 308,888 troops were transported by British ships; French histories report 48,474 were carried by French ships, 26,314 of these directly to French ports.

When the 108,982 Tommies arrived at Dover (according to V. Adm. Ramsay's 'Dover Report'; 77,605 also arrived at smaller ports from Margate to Brighton) their journey was not yet over. Most of the ships docked two to three deep at the port's eight cross-Channel berths at the Admiralty Pier where the disembarking troops were counted by Landing Control (annotating names and units) and crossed 200m (656ft) to the trains waiting at the Marine Station. Alerted three days prior, by 23 May the Railway Executive Committee had assembled 186 ten-coach troop trains from the Southern, Great Western, London, Midland and Scottish, and London North Eastern railways and established a joint military–civilian control centre at Redhill, Surrey.

The men were transported to large military camps west of London – at Aldershot, Blandford, Dorchester, Oxford, Tetbury and Tidworth – in an impressively immense and efficient railway operation. For the French there was no time for rest. Leaving behind approximately 6,000 dead and 40,000

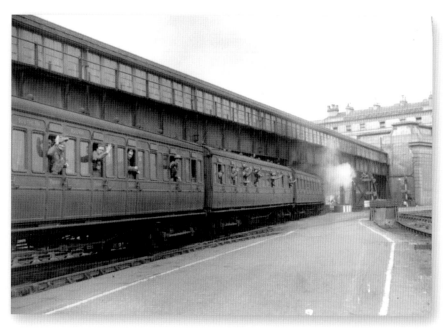

Upon arriving at port, Dunkirk's survivors were transported by an aggressive and robust railways system to six different military camps. After a short rest they would be regrouped and units reconstituted and prepared to return to war. (IWM H1657)

Reconstitution and redeployment of British and French Forces, June

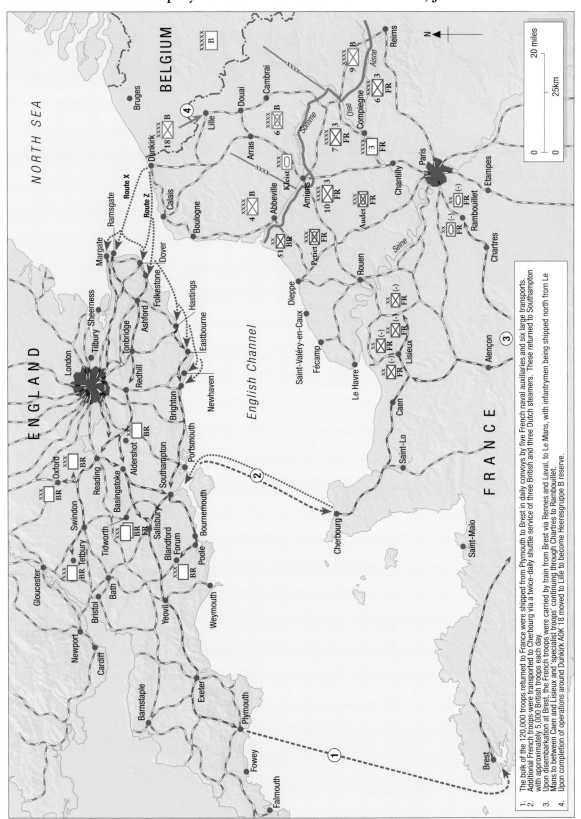

1. The bulk of the 120,000 troops returned to France were shipped from Plymouth to Brest in daily convoys by five French naval auxiliaries and six large transports. Additional French troops were transported to Cherbourg via a twice-daily shuttle service of three British and three Dutch steamers. These returned to Southampton with approximately 5,000 British troops each day.
2. Upon disembarkation at Brest, the French troops were carried by train from Brest via Rennes and Laval, to Le Mans, with infantrymen being shipped north from Le Mans to between Caen and Lisieux and 'specialist troops' continuing through Chartres to Rambouillet.
3. Upon completion of operations around Dunkirk AOK 18 moved to Lille to become Heeresgruppe B reserve.

captured at Dunkirk, some 122,000 French troops were evacuated to British ports. They arrived exhausted, hungry, demoralized and were immediately disarmed by British military police (*un affront injustifié* – though disembarking Tommies were as well) before being herded onto trains. They were taken by rail to Salisbury then to the nearby Tidworth army camp. There they were fed, clothed and briefly billeted in the 30,000-man camp, 20 schools in Southampton and individual homes in three neighbouring towns.

While roughly 2,000 of them remained in Britain on account of wounds or for other reasons, the rest were quickly returned to France to continue the fight. Less than 48 hours after arriving in England, most were transported to Southampton and Plymouth for their voyage home. (Some of the *poilus* were taken from disembarkation directly to these two ports, resulting in a stay of less than 24 hours). From Plymouth the five small Élan-class dispatch boats and six large (5,800-/10,172-ton) transports ferried most of them to Brest. From Southampton three British and three Dutch ships shuttled others to Cherbourg (from where they returned with about 5,000 Tommies on each run).

From the French ports some 100,000 infantrymen and artillerists were moved to the region between Caen and the Seine to be reformed into divisions. Although they were in terrible shape, had to be rearmed and were hopelessly mixed in units from 17 different divisions, Gén. Georges attempted to create a corps of four divisions from them. The 'specialists' from the *divisions légères mécaniques* were regrouped south-west of Paris, received new equipment directly from the factories and formed two small mechanized divisions. However, by this time the Panzers were overrunning the rest of France and fewer than half saw combat against Germany again.

In total, *Dynamo* and the evacuations preceding it brought home 221,504 British troops. Within three weeks Operations *Aerial* and *Cycle* evacuated another 144,171 south of the Somme, mostly men of the BEF's rear area logistics personnel but also those of the 1st Armoured (but only 21 tanks), 52nd (Lowland) and 1st Canadian Divisions. The remaining BEF formation

– the 51st (Highland) Division – was captured intact at Saint-Valéry-en-Caux on 12 June while awaiting evacuation. Adding to these the nearly 10,000 troops withdrawn from Norway meant the British had sufficient numbers to man 16 infantry divisions, but it would take three weeks to reconstitute the BEF divisions. Even then it was possible to equip fully only three of them. For example, there were only 54 anti-tank guns, 420 field guns and 163 heavy guns available in the UK. While lacking hardware, Britain had the huge benefit of recovering the core of the professional army and this cadre had the benefit of being experienced in the horrors, rigours and requisites of modern mobile combat.

While successful, *Dynamo* was a costly operation, especially for the naval forces. By the time it ended at 1423hrs on 4 June the Allies had lost 240 vessels with another 45 badly damaged. Most grievous of course were Royal Navy and French destroyer losses. Six British and three French warships of this category were sunk and 26 damaged.

For the RAF *Dynamo* was an expensive learning experience. A close examination of Luftwaffe loss reports and unit operational records reveals that British fighters destroyed 42 bombers and 36 fighters over Dunkirk. (Additionally, four Stukas and two Ju 88s are known to have fallen to ships' anti-aircraft fire.) In return Air Vice-Marshal Park's 11 Group lost 84 fighters to Messerschmitts and bombers' defensive fire, thus costing more than one fighter for each enemy aircraft downed. Fighter Command's front-line strength was reduced to only 331 Spitfires and Hurricanes with 36 in reserve. However, the traumatic and costly experience paid off – as much as the advantage of radar – in the RAF's victory over the Luftwaffe in the Battle of Britain.

But regardless of the cost to the Royal Navy and RAF Operation *Dynamo* was a success – and a crucial element in the eventual Allied defeat of Nazi Germany – even if it did not constitute a victory over the Wehrmacht. As Churchill so rightly stated, 'We must be very careful not to assign to this deliverance the attributes of victory. Wars are not won by evacuations.'

THE BATTLEFIELD TODAY

Seventy years separate today from the titanic struggle that took place at Dunkirk, Bray-Dunes, La Panne and Nieuport in the climactic events of the late spring, 1940. As is all too common, the ground upon which men fought and died – or escaped and lived to fight another day – has been masked by the ever-expanding spread of growing civilization, nurtured by the six and a half decades of peace that followed. This is made even more marked by the need to rebuild almost everything following destruction experienced in 1940 and the even greater devastation suffered during the stubborn German defence of the area four years later.

Consequently, Dunkirk itself has been almost completely transformed and the inner port area replaced with a new one of a whole new design. The outer harbour, however, remains virtually unchanged. The most prominent feature – the 1,280m-long (4,200ft) east mole – still stands, but concrete pilings have replaced the original timber ones. Access is easy and the walk out gives pause when one considers that some 239,555 men were saved from this harbour. The gangway goes approximately 800m (2,600ft) out, the Germans having blown a gap in the jetty to ensure that any Allied commandos would have to disembark within machine-gun range of the bunkers at the base of the 'mole'.

Looking back at Dunkirk from the end of the 800m (875-yard) concrete walkway mounted atop the east mole jetty. Dunkirk now rests peacefully, most of its skyline – centred on the spires of the Saint Eloi cathedral – restored and expanded in the seven decades since Dynamo. (Author's collection)

Several memorials commemorate the events and sacrifice at Dunkirk, Bray-Dunes and De Panne during those traumatic days of May and June 1940. The main one is located at the base of the East Mole and glorifies the sacrifice of the Allied aviators, sailors and soldiers during the Bataille de Dunkerque. The steps in the background lead to the east mole, the end of which, with its tiny white lighthouse, may be seen extending into the far distance. (Author's collection)

Indeed one of the difficulties with identifying Allied defences is the fact that the Germans spent four years fortifying the area, all the while expecting the Allies' return to happen next door at Calais. Consequently care must be taken to prevent confusing defences constructed by the Nazis for those originally built by the French.

Vice-amiral Abrial's HQ – the famous Bastion 32 – may be visited, its cavernous gun galleries now housing the Dynamo-Dunkerque Mémorial du Souvenir (www.dynamo-dunkerque.com) and museum. Though small it is well stocked and well worth the visit. Similarly the impressive exterior of Fort des Dunes, from which Gén. Janssen directed the defence of the beachhead's eastern sector after the departure of II Corps, can be viewed but it is closed to visitors.

Moving east down the beaches the pleasant peaceful seaside hotels belie the horrific contest that took place on these beaches. The suburban sprawl of a now expansive Malo-les-Bains has overrun the dunes in which the last redoubt of British defenders bivouacked during their last night on French soil. Further east the central portion of the Vancauwenberghe Sanatorium, a landmark for arriving ships, remains original but the wings are post-war reconstruction and considerably shorter.

Bray-Dunes has many new hotels lining the sea front promenade but the occasional original building still lends a whiff of the town's 1940s atmosphere. The pre-war bandstand – the reporting point for embarking troops – has been rebuilt as an overlook mounting a large marble memorial to the heroic defence of the 12e Division d'infanterie motorisée. and smaller brass plaques commemorating the loss of the destroyer *Bourrasque* and submarine *Doris* (pre-*Dynamo*).

At De Panne the bandstand is replaced by a similar beach overlook, this one sporting a Belgian flag. The site of King Albert's Koninklyke Villa, destroyed during the fighting in 1944, now supports a massive Belgian memorial to King Léopold I.

FURTHER READING

Much has been written about Dunkirk but few have attempted to incorporate the many sides (four nations in conflict and all facets: air, land and sea) of the whole story. Therefore a compendium of previous publications must be studied to provide a comprehensive understanding of the events filling those traumatic days.

It is best to begin with the official British military histories: Major Lionel Frederic Ellis's *The War in France and Flanders 1939–1940* (HMSO: London, 1954) and the Royal Navy's *Naval Staff History – Battle Summary No. 41* originally compiled and edited in 1949 by W. J. R. Gardner but reprinted (as *The Evacuation from Dunkirk: Operation Dynamo*, (Frank Cass Publishers: London, 2000) without changes.

While national bias dramatically colours British military histories, the Germans almost universally saw Dunkirk as a 'sideshow' and hence it is largely unreported in German publications. For appreciating the German Army perspective, see Telford Taylor's *March of Conquest: German Victories in Western Europe, 1940* (Simon and Schuster: New York, 1958).

Because *Dynamo* was such an iconic British military experience many books cover the horrific human experience of having participated in or been rescued by the operation. Arguably the best at this is American historian Walter Lord in his *The Miracle of Dunkirk* (Viking Press: New York, 1982).

Few of these popular histories focus on the maritime side of the operation, the best being David Devine's *The Nine Days of Dunkirk* (W. W. Norton & Company: New York, Inc., 1959). Having captained a 30ft Thames motor cruiser in the evacuation, Devine provides by far the most detailed and nautical description of the maritime operations.

The best account of French participation in the campaign and their own evacuation is Jacques Mordal's *Dunkerque* (Éditions France-Empire: Paris, 1968). Much more useful for the English-only reader is François de Lannoy's *Dunkerque 1940* (Editions Heimdal: Bayeux, 2004). While the narrative is French, the concise text uses readily recognizable military terms and unit designations, and the abundance of maps, charts, photos and sidebars make it easily understandable.

Air power played a key roll in the campaign but is largely under-represented in literature. All the above-mentioned references use aggregate figures and daily summary 'box scores' to represent the aerial contest. At a more detailed level, telling the RAF's side of the story is Norman Franks' *Air Battle Dunkirk, 26 May–3 June 1940* (Grub Street: London, 2000).

For real information regarding the units, engagements and losses occurring in the nine days of air combat over Dunkirk, study the excellent *The Battle of France Then and Now* (Battle of Britain International Ltd: Old Harlow, 2007) by Peter D. Cornwell.

Finally, the most balanced and informative overall account – though still without significant detail from the German side – is Robert Jackson's *Dunkirk: The British Evacuation, 1940* (Arthur Barker: London, 1976).

For the serious student of this grand, multi-faceted contest, all of the books mentioned below are highly recommended.

Belgium: *The Official Account of What Happened, 1939–1940* (Evans Brothers Limited: London, 1941)

Battistelli, Pier Paolo, Battle Orders 32: *Panzer Divisions: The Blitzkrieg Years 1939–40* (Osprey Publishing Ltd: Oxford, 2007)

Bekker, Cajus, *The Luftwaffe War Diaries: The German Air Force in World War II* (Doubleday & Company: New York, 1968)

Benoist-Méchin, Jacques, *Sixty Days that Shook the West: The Fall of France, 1940* translated by Peter Wiles (G. P. Putnam's Sons: New York, 1963)

Bingham, Victor F., *'Blitzed!' The Battle of France, May–June 1940* (Air Research Publications: Walton on Thames, 1990)

Boatner, Mark M., III, *The Biographical Dictionary of World War II* (Presidio Press: Novato, CA, 1996)

Bond, Brian, *France and Belgium 1939–1940* (Associated University Presses, Inc.: Cranbury, NJ, 1979)

Caldwell, Donald, *The JG 26 War Diary, Volume One 1939–1942* (Grub Street: London, 1996)

Churchill, Winston S., *The Second World War, Volume II Their Finest Hour* (Cassell & Co. Ltd.: London, 1949)

Coastal Command: The Air Ministry Account of the Part Played by Coastal Command in the Battle of the Seas, 1939–1942 (The MacMillan Company: New York, 1943)

Collier, Richard, *The Sands of Dunkirk* (E. P. Dutton & Co., Ltd: New York, 1961)

Cornwell, Peter D., *The Battle of France Then and Now* (Battle of Britain International Ltd: Old Harlow, 2007)

Corum, James S., 'The Other Richthofen', *World War II*, Vol. 23, No. 3, August/September 2008

Dallies-Labourdette, Jean-Philippe, *S-Boote: German E-boats in action (1939–1945)* trans. Janice Lert (Histoire et Collections: Paris, 2003)

Divine, David, *The Nine Days of Dunkirk* (W. W. Norton & Company, Inc.: New York, 1959)

'Dunkirk Evacuation', *After the Battle* No. 3, August 1973, Battle of Britain International Ltd, pp. 13-21

Ellis, Major L. F., *The War in France and Flanders 1939–1940* (HMSO: London, 1954)

Franks, Norman L. R., *Air Battle Dunkirk, 26 May–3 June 1940* (Grub Street: London, 2000)

Gardner, W. J. R., ed.,*The Evacuation from Dunkirk: Operation Dynamo, 26 May–4 June 1940* (Frank Cass Publishers: London, 2000)

Gardner, W. J. R., 'The Death of Admiral Ramsay', *After the Battle* No. 87, August 1995, Battle of Britain International Ltd, pp. 44–53

Gelb, Norman, *Dunkirk: The Complete Story of the First Step in the Defeat of Hitler* (William Morrow and Company, Inc.: New York, 1989)

Guderian, General Heinz, *Panzer Leader* trans. Constantine Fitzgibbon (E. P. Dutton & Co., Inc.: New York, 1952)

Hooten, E. R., *Phoenix Triumphant: The Rise and Rise of the Luftwaffe* (Arms & Armour Press: London, 1994)

Horne, Alistair, *To Lose A Battle: France, 1940* (Little, Brown and Company: Boston, 1969)

Jackson, Robert, *Air War over France 1939–40* (Ian Allan Ltd: London, 1974)

—, *Dunkirk: The British Evacuation, 1940* (Arthur Barker: London, 1976)

Kesselring, Field-Marshal Albert, *The Memoirs of Field-Marshal Kesselring*, translation of *Soldat bis zum letzten Tag* by William Kimber Ltd (Presido Press: Novato, CA, 1989)

Kindell, Don, *British and Other Navies in World War 2*, May 1940, Part 4, and June 1940, Part 1 as published on website: http://www.naval-history.net/xDKWW2-4005-14MAY04.htm and http://www.naval-history.net/xDKWW2-4006-19JUN01.htm

Lannoy, François de, *Dunkerque 1940* (Editions Heimdal: Bayeux, 2004)

Looseley, Rhiannon, 'Le Paradis après l'Enfer: the French Soldiers Evacuated from Dunkirk in 1940', *History Today*, Vol. 56, June 2006

Lord, Walter, *The Miracle of Dunkirk* (Viking Press: New York, 1982)

Macksey, Kenneth, *Guderian: Panzer General* (Greenhill Books/Lionel Leventhal Ltd: London, 2003)

Nafziger, George F., *The German Order of Battle: Infantry in World War II* (Greenhill Books, Lionel Leventhal Ltd: London, 2000)

Nafziger, George F., *The German Order of Battle: Panzers and Artillery in World War II* (Greenhill Books, Lionel Leventhal Ltd: London, 1999)

Powaski, Ronald E., *Lightning War: Blitzkrieg in the West, 1940* (Castle Books: Edison, NJ, 2006)

Ritgen, Oberst a.D. Helmut, Vanguard 2: *The 6th Panzer Division 1937–45* (Osprey Publishing Ltd: London, 1982)

Sebag-Montefiore, Hugh, *Dunkirk: Fight to the Last Man* (Harvard University Press: Cambridge, MA, 2006)

Shirer, William L., *The Collapse of the Third Republic: An Inquiry into the Fall of France in 1940* (Simon and Schuster: New York, 1969)

Smith, Peter C., *Stuka: Luftwaffe Dive-Bomber Units 1939–1941* (Ian Allan Ltd: London, 2006)

—, *Stuka Sqn.: Stukagruppe 77 – the Luftwaffe's 'Fire Brigade'* (Patrick Stephens Ltd: Wellingborough, 1990)

Tarnstrom, Ronald L., *French Arms* (Trogen Books: Lindsborg, KA, 2001)

Taylor, Telford, *March of Conquest*: *The German Victories in Western Europe, 1940* (Simon and Schuster: New York, 1958)

Whitley, M. J., *Destroyers of World War Two: An International Encyclopedia* (Naval Institute Press: Annapolis, MD, 2002)

Williamson, Gordon, New Vanguard 59: *German E-boats 1939–45* (Osprey Publishing Ltd: Oxford, 2002)

INDEX

Figures in **bold** refer to illustrations

Aa Canal, crossing of 6, 20, 29, 37
AA cruisers: *Calcutta* 37, 52, 78, 79
Abrial, Vice-amiral Jean-Charles 12, **12**, 13, 16, 36, 81, 91
Advanced Air Striking Force (RAF) 18
Adam, Lt. Gen. Sir Ronald 27, 63
Aéronavale, mission flown by 75
aircraft 36, 69, 74
    Avro Anson 49, **73**, 74
    Blackburn Skua 64
    Boulton Paul Defiant 18, **40**, 41, **49**, **66–7**, 68, 69
    Bristol Blenheim 18, 64, 78
    Dornier Do 17Z 21, 36, 41, 74, 79
    Fairey Albacore 64
    Fairey Swordfish 49, **49**, 64
    Hawker Hurricane 18, 30, **34**, 36, **40**, 41, 9, 52, 64, 68, 69, 74, 75, 78, 79, 80, 89
    Heinkel He 111 21, 49, **66–7**, 68, 74, 78
    Junkers Ju 87 Stuka 13, 14, **20**, 21, 36, **49**, 52, 53, **54–5**, 56, **71**, **72**, 74, 75, 78, 79, 89
    Junkers Ju 88A **20**, 36, 43, 49, **49**, 52, 74, 79, 89
    Lockheed Hudson **72**, **88**
    Messerschmitt Bf 109E **18**, 36, **40**, 41, 49, **49**, 64, 68, 69, 74, 75, 78, 79, 80, 89
    Messerschmitt Bf 110C **34**, **49**, 74, 78
    Supermarine Spitfire 18, **18**, 30, **34**, 36, **40**, 41, 44, 68, 74, 78, 89
    Vought 156F 75
    Westland Lysander 64, 74, 78
Alexander, Maj. Gen. The Hon. Harold 53, 63, **65**, 73, 80
anti-submarine trawlers, use of 76, 78, 79
Ardennes Forest, Panzers in **4**, 5
armed minesweeping trawlers, use of 57
    Calvi **54–5**, 56, 57
armed yachts, use of 71, 80
Armée de l'Air 18, 20, 80
Armentières 38, 39, 57
army assault landing craft, use of 52, 72
army motor craft, use of 71
Arras, fight for 6–7, 19
auxiliary minesweepers 36, 75, 85

barges, use of 30, 71
Barthélemy, Gén. Eugène 16, 32, 81, 85
Barwell, Plt. Off. E. G. **66–7**, 68
Basse Colme Canal 53, 60, 73, 76
Beaufrère, Gén. 27, 76, 85
Belgian Army 13, 14, 33–4, **33**
    in action 15, 29, 33–4, **33**, 44
    retreat and surrender 7, 38, 39, 40
Belgium 30, 33–4, **38**, 39, 73
    Allied forces in **5**, 6, 13, **15**, 16, 19
    German advance in 5–6, 14, 19, 39
    surrender of 40
Bergues, defence of 15, 16, 27, **49**, 53, 63, 73, 76, 77, 78–9
Béthune, BEF forces at **12**, 19, 32
Blanchard, Gén. 16, 29, 34, 43, 65
Bock, Generaloberst Feodor von 7, 20, 33
Bollezeele, fighting at 32, 37–8, 49, **49**

Boulogne 6, 7, 14, 16, 29, 45
Bourbourg, fighting at 6, 16, 32, 38, 64, 80
Bray-Dunes, evacuations from 27, **39**, 53, 65, 71, 72, 73, 74, 91
Brest, French troops return to 88
Bridgeman, Lt. Col. Lord 6, 7, 27
British Expeditionary Force (BEF) 5
    actions/deployment of **5**, 6, 7, 15, 19, 27, **28**, 29, 31, 32, 33, 34, 37, 38, 39, 40, 43, 44, **46–7**, 48, 52, 53, 60, 62, **62**, 63, 64, 73, 77, 78, 79, 80, 88
    evacuation of 7, 27, 30, 34, 37, 40, **54–5**, 56, 62, 63, **65**, 72, **73**, 77, 78, **79**, 80, 88
    motorized transport **5**, **15**, 39, 40, 88
    numbers evacuated from **44**, 45, 52, 63, 65, 72, 79, **79**, 80, 84, 85, 88, 90
    order of battle (30 May) 22–3
    retreat of forces 4, 6, 7, 15, **15**, 27, 29, 8–9, 40, 44, 53, 62, **65**, 73, 76, 77
    troops' anger at lack of ships 62, **65**
    troops lost at sea **54–5**, 56, 74
Brooke, Lt. Gen. Alan F. 7, 11, 72

Calais 6, 7, 14, 29, 36, **73**
Canal des Chats, defence of 73, 76
Canal des Moëres 78, 79, 80, 85
Canal Line, Panzers advance 15, 19, 20, 32
car ferries: *Autocarrier* 81
cargo/stores/supply ships, use of 43, 45
Cassel, assault on 32, 44, **46–7**, 48, 53, 62
Cherbourg, evacuations from 36, 75, 88
Churchill, PM Winston 4, 5, 34, 89
coastal freighters: *Aboukir* 21
'coasters'/'motor coaster' 30, 36, 45, 65, 71
Comines–Ypres Canal, defence of 29, 34, 38, 43, 53

destroyers, use of 17, 36, 37, 43, 45, 52, 57, **57**, 60, 63, **69**, 71, 72, **72**, 74, 75, 76, 77, **77**, 79, 80, 81, 84, 80
    Basilisk 74; *Bourrasque* 60, **91**; *Cyclone* 52, **63**, 65; *Express* 84; *Foudroyant* 75; *Grafton* **17**, **50–1**; *Grenade* **54–5**, 56; *Havant* 74; *Ivanhoe* 74; *Jaguar* 21; *Keith* 72, 74; *Léopard* 80; *Mistral* 52; *Sabre* 56; *Shikari* **84–5**; *Vanquisher* **30**, 63, **69**; *Venomous* 80; *Verity* **54–5**, 56; *Vivacious* **57**, 71; *Wakeful* **17**, **50–1**; *Whitshed* 77; *Winchelsea* 77
Deule Canal, defence of 29, 39
Dinant, German breakthrough at 6, 15
dispatch boats, use of 52, 63, **64**, 78, 88
Dover 45, 57, 72
    ships sail to 30, 52, **64**, 65, 77, 79, 86
    troops unloaded at **64**, 77, 81, 86
drifters 37, **44**, 45, 63, 71, 75, 77, 80, 81, 84
Dunkirk, evacuation from 7, **30**
    air defence of 40, 41, 80
    assessment of as unusable 37, 57, **61**
    bombardment/bombing/mining of 31, 36, 37, 40, **44**, 49, 53, **54–5**, 56, 64, **64**, 65, 69, 71, 74, 75, **75**, 77
    daytime hazards **54–5**, 56, 65, 77
    disposition of forces around **42**
    embarkation facilities 27, 37, **58–9**

evacuation from **30**, 41, 43, 45, 52, 57, **57**, **61**, 62, 63, **65**, 69, **69**, 72, **73**, 76, 77, **77**, **78**, **79**, 80, 81, 84–5
    evacuation points **58–9**
    halt to embarkations 65, 75
    last vessels leave 77, 80, 81, 84–5
    numbers evacuated from **44**, 45, 52, 63, 65, 72, 79, **79**, 80, 84, 85, 88, 90
    surviving features of 90, **90**, **91**
    temporary closing of 57, 75, 85
    troops left behind 76, 77, **84**
Dunkirk–Lille Pocket, defence of 15, 16, 18, 20, 27, **28**, 29, 31, 37–8, 40
Dunkirk perimeter 13, 27, 52, 53
    attacks on 41, 44, 45, **58–9**, 60, 64, **64**, 70, 71, 76, 78, 80, **82–3**, 85
    defence of 29, 37, 38, 40, 45, **58–9**, 62, 64, 80, **82–3**, 85
Dyle Line/River, forces on **5**, 15, **15**

English Channel
    evacuation routes (X, Y and Z) 35, **35**, 36–7, 45, 57, **60**, 61, 75, 78
    mines in 21, 36, 37, 57, **60**, 63, 85
Ervine-Andrews, Capt. H. M. VC 76, **76**

Fagalde, Gén. M. B. Alfred **12**, 13, 15, 16, 27, 32, 63, 73, 80, 81
Fall Gelb (*Case Yellow*) 14, 20, 31
Fall Rot (*Case Red*) 31, 45, 52, 60, 69
fast launches, use of 71
fishing boats, use of 63, 65, 71, 80, 81
Fleet Air Arm, attacks by 49, **49**, 64
Forest of Nieppe, BEF troops in 38, 44
Fortune, Maj. Gen. Sir Victor Morven **12**
Franklyn, Maj. Gen. Harold E. 29, 34, **34**, 38, 39, 43, 62, 72
French Army
    actions/deployment of 6, 7, 13, 15, 16, **16**, 18, 27, **28**, 29, 32, **33**, 37–8, 39, 40, 41, 45, 52, 57, 60, 62, 63, 64, 73, 76, 78, 79, 80, 81, 88
    evacuation of 34, 45, 63, 65, 74, 75, 76, **77**, 81, 85, 88
    numbers left behind 80, **84**, 85
    order of battle (30 May) 24
    reformation/redeployment of **87**, 88
    retreat of 18, 29, 32, 34, 38, 39
French Navy ('Pas de Calais flotilla') 24
    attacks on ships 21, 52, **63**, 65, 89, 91
    evacuation by 52, 63, **64**, 65, 80, 86
frontier line, defence of 73, 76, 78
Furnes, fighting at 27, 36, 53, 60, 64, **64**, 75

Georges, Gén. Alphonse-Joseph 11, 88
German Army
    actions/deployment of 5–7, 15, 19, 20, 21, 31, 32, 33, **33**, 37, **37**, 38, **38**, 39, 40, 41, 43, **43**, 44, 45, **46–7**, 48, 49, 52–3, 57, 60, **60**, 61, 62, **62**, 64, **64**, 65, 69, 71, 75, 76, 78–9, 80, 85
    order of battle (30 May) 25
    Panzers, advance of 5, 14, 19, 20, 32, 37–8, **37**, 44, 45, 53, 80
    realignment/restructuring of 52, 61
Göring, Reichsmarschall 14, 21, 31, 74

Gort, Gen. Lord 6, 7, 11–12, **11**, 13, 15, 27, 2**9**, 34, 40, 43, 53, 72
Gravelines, fighting for 15, 16, 19, 27, 36, 38, 45, 49, **75**
Guderian, Gen. Heinz W. 5, 6, 14, 19, 32, **33**, 37–8, 45, 60, 80

Herseaux, BEF forces pass through 5
Hitler, Adolf 13, 19, 20, 21, 31, 32, 40, 52
Holland, supply of *schuyts* 30
hospital carriers 36, 45, 63, 65, 76, 79
  Paris 79; *Worthing* 79
Hoymille, fighting near 53, 76, 78
Hunter, Sqn. Ldr. Philip A. **66–7**, 68

Irwin, Maj. Gen. Noel 38, 53
Iseghem, penetration at 33, 39

Janssen, Général 73, 78, 91

Kalischewski, Oblt. Robert **66–7**, 68
King, LAC F. H. **66–7**, 68
Kleist, Gen. Ewald von 19, 20, 60
Kluge, Generaloberst Günther Hans von 19, 20, 32, 60
Kriegsmarine (German Navy) 21, 65, 76
  anti-shipping operations 20, **20**, 21, 36, 45, **49**, **50–1**, 57, 63, 65, **65**, **73**, 76
  order of battle (30 May) 26
  S-boats **20**, 21, 36, 45, 49, **50–1**, 57, 63, 65, **73**, 76
  U-boats 21, **50–1**, **73**
Küchler, Gen. Georg von 5, 13, **13**, 20, **33**, 61, **64**, 71, 75, 76, 78–9

La Bassée Canal, action at 15, 33, **37**, 38
La Panne, evacuations from 27, 52, 57, 62, 71, 72, **72**
Laurencie, Gén. 39, 41, 62
Léopold III, King of the Belgians 33, 34, **37**, 40, 91
Les Moëres inundation/salient 62, 73, 76
lifeboats, use of 41, 45, **65**, **69**, 71
lighthouse tender, use of 37
Lille, fight for 14, 38, 39, 41, **42**, 65
'little ships', use of **29**, 30, 37, **44**, 52, 57, **60**, 65, 71, 72, 77, 80
Luftwaffe 14
  anti-shipping operations **20**, 36, 43, 52, 53, 57, 65, **71**, 74, 75, 79
  bombing operations 16, **20**, 31, 36, 40, **40**, 41, 49, 52, **54–5**, 56, 65, **66–7**, 68, 69, 74, 78, 79, 89
  dive-bombing operations 13, 14, 21, 36, 41, 49, **49**, 52, **54–5**, 56, **71**, 74, 78, 79
  effects of weather on operations 31, 41, 45, 49, 61
  fighter operations 30, **34**, 40, 41, 49, 52, 64, 69, 74, 75, 78, 79, 80, 89
  order of battle (30 May) 25–6
Lys Canal/River, defence of 15, 29, 32, 3, 39, 53

Malo-les-Bains, evacuations from 27, 52, 53, 71, 76, 77, 80, 81, 91
Manstein, Generalfeldmarschall Erich von **13**
Margate, troops return to 79, 86
Martel, Maj. Gen. Giffard **29**, 44, 62, 73
mines, use of 36, 45, **53**, 57, **60**, 63, 79, 85

minesweepers of 30, 37, 45, 52, 56, 57, 63, **64**, 72, **72**, 74, 75, 77, 80, 81, 84, 85
  Albury 85; *Hebe* 72; *Kellet* 84; *Skipjack* 74
Mont des Cats, defence of 44, 53
Montgomery, Maj. Gen. Bernard L. 39, 44, 60, 72
motor anti-submarine boats 72, 80
motor torpedo boats, use of 81, 84
motor vessels/yachts, use of 36, 75
motorboats **29**, 30, 45, 63, 71, 72, 81
motorized 'X lighters', use of 71

Nieuport
  fighting at 27, 36, **38**, 40, 52–3, 64, 76
  German artillery fire from 57, **60**, **75**
Nieuport Canal, bombing of bridges 64
Noordschote, defence of 39, 44, 53

observation balloons, use of 71
OKH, actions of 19, 20, 31, 32, **33**, 52, 61
OKW, actions of 19, 21, 32, 34, 52
Operation *Dynamo*
  Admiralty signal to commence 36
  aims/planning and preparation 27, 29
  near derailment of 57
  number of ships involved 86
Osborne, Maj. Gen. Edmund 44, 52, 53

packet steamers, use of 30
  Fenella **54–5**, 56; *Mona's Queen* 53
paddle minesweepers 30, 37, 52, **65**, 72, 75
  Brighton Queen 75; *Devonia* 65
patrol sloops, use of 52, 65, 81
  Bideford 52; *Widgeon* 65, 76
personnel ships **29**, 30, 36, 37, 41, **41**, 43, 45, 52, 63, 65, **65**, 71, 77, 80, 81, 84
  Crested Eagle **54–5**, 56, **65**
Pont-aux-Cerfs bridge, crossing of 53, 62
Portsmouth Inner Patrol, yachts from 71
Pound, First Sea Lord Sir Dudley 57, 63

RAF seaplane tender motorboats 71, 79
railway steamers, use of 30, 36, 74, 75
  Prague 74; *Scotia* 75
railways, transport of troops 86, **86**, 88
Ramsay, V. Adm. Bertram 6, 12, **12**, 17, 29, 30, 36, 37, 45, 57, 63, 65, 71, 77, 80, 81, 86, **88**
Ramsgate, use of port 30, 71, **81**
Reynaud, Premier Paul 5, 34
Richthofen, Generalmajor Wolfram von 13–14, **13**, **20**, 21, 31, 52, 69
Rommel, General Erwin **37**, 38
Royal Air Force operations
  Army Cooperation Command 64, 74, 78
  Bomber Command 18, 23, 64, 78
  Coastal Command 24, 49, **72**, **73**, 74, **88**
  Fighter Command 18, **18**, 23, 27, 30, **34**, 36, **40**, 41, 49, **49**, 52, 61, 64, 68, 69, 74, 75, 77, 78, 79, 80, 89
  order of battle (30 May) 23–4
Royal Daffodil, attack on 79
Royal Naval Reserve 30
Royal Navy (Dover Command) 57, 74
  berthing parties, role of 43
  control team, return of to England 80
  Landing Control, work of 86

losses 17, **17**, **20**, 45, 52, **54–5**, 56, 57, 71, 74, 79, 89
mining/anti-mine operations 17, 36, 37
order of battle (30 May) 23
pier parties, role of 79, 81, 84
ships/vessels for evacuation 12, 17, **17**, **20**, 23, 27, **29**, 30, 34, 36, **41**, 43, 45, 2, **4–5**, 56, 57, 71, 74, 79, 81, **81**, 89
shore parties 37, 57, 63, 72
withdrawal of destroyers from 57
Rundstedt, Generaloberst Gerd von 19, 20, 21, 52, 60

Saint-Omer, forces at 6, 16, 19, 36
Saint-Pol oil refinery, burning of **30**, 36
Scheldt Estuary, crossing of 13, 20, 21
schuyts, use of 30, 37, 45, 57, 63, 71, **72**, 77, 80, 81, **81**, 84
Small Vessels Pool (SVP) 30, 71
Somerset, Brig. Nigel F. 53, 62
Southampton, French troops leave 88
Spycker, German advance on 27, 78
steamers 30, 36, **41**, 45, 52, 65, 81, 85
  Ain el Turk 65; *King George V* 85; *Queen of the Channel* 41, **41**, 43, 45

tanks 14, 20, 34, **46–7**, 48, 88
  H35 80; PzKpfw II **37**, 48; PzKpfw III 78; PzKpfw IV 48, 78; PzKpfw 35(t) **4**, **43**, 44, **46–7**, 48; S35 62, 78, 80; Vickers Mk VI **88**
Tennant RN, Capt. William G. **36**, 37, 41, 43, 45, 57, 76, 77, 80
Thames Estuary Defence Flotilla 74
  Locust 74; *Mosquito* 74
Thorne, Maj. Gen. Andrew 27, 44
torpedo boat destroyers: (*Siroco*) 63, 65
torpedo boats, use of 17, 63, 65, 80
  Bouclier 65
trawlers, use of **54–5**, 56, 65, **72**, 75, 81, 84
  Arley 56; *Brock* 56; *Cattling John* **54–5**, 56; *Fyldea* **54–5**, 56; *Pacifico* 85; *Polly Johnson* **54–5**, 56
tugs 30, 45, 52, 63, 65, 71, **72**, 74, 80, 81, 84
  Goliath 84; *St Abbs* 74; *St Helier* 80

Wake-Walker, Rear Adm. William F. 57, 62–3, 74, 80, 81
Wason RA, Maj. Gen. S. R. 29, 62
Watten, fight for 32, 37
weaponry
  anti-aircraft guns 17, **17**, 38, **39**, 40, 41, 44, 53, **69**, 77, 89
  anti-tank guns 5, 16, 48, 77
  artillery 16, **19**, 20, 27, 33, **33**, 34, 36, 38, **38**, 39, 40, 44, 45, **46–7**, 52, 53, 57, 60, **62**, 65, 71, 75, 75, 78, 89
  machine guns 17, **33**, 40, **46–7**, 48, 53, **66–7**, 68, **69**, 74, 80
  rifles 44, **62**
  torpedoes **17**, **20**, **50–1**, **63**, 65
Westende, Fleet Air Arm bombing of 64
Weygand, Gén. Maxime 6, 34
Wietersheim, Gen. Gustav von 45, 60
Williams, Plt. Off. J. E. M. **66–7**, 68

Yarmouth Base, drifters from 71
Ypres, defence of 6, 33, 34, 39, 64
Yser River, defences on 40, 44, 53, **64**, 71